2021

David,

Merry Christmas!

— Gary

HE'S ONE OF US

One Officer's Strategy for Making a Difference

———————

Jim Ferree

HE'S ONE OF US

To all the Sheepdogs:
Those who willingly stand in the presence of danger, protecting those who otherwise would fall prey…

Society needs you to stand strong, your family needs you remain safe and sane, and your church community needs you to personify consistent courage.

Table of Contents

Foreword

As a Pastor for over 30 years and service to Law Enforcement in the capacity of Chaplain dating back over 28 years, I have enjoyed and appreciated the symbiotic bond between pastors and police officers. Perhaps it's found in a calling that leads to servant leadership and sacrifice. Maybe it is the heightened sense of right and wrong they both feel. Or it could be the desire to protect others from dangers that cause harm or even death. In any case, I have known pastors that became police officers and police officers that became pastors. Both begin with the desire to make a difference and help save people from harm that comes their way. And both direct them to the safety that brings peace in a chaotic and dangerous world.

Jim Ferree is both a Pastor and Police officer. He began his pursuit of God and his higher calling as a skeptic. But he found himself with a unique view from inside the church and on the streets of Phoenix. Drawing from both of these worlds, Jim invites us to join him in an academy of action, sharing both knowledge and insight that invites us into the challenging, exciting, difficult, and sacrificial world of living with a clear understanding of a shared calling and commissioning.

If you are willing to engage these pages with humility and willingness to learn, Jim will show you how to understand the authority God has given you. He will demonstrate how to humbly be a servant leader, standing firm, unafraid, and unwilling to back down in God's truth. Most importantly, Jim will show you how to live life in the way it is meant to be lived.

Jim's honest, transparent, and engaging stories of successes, sacrifices, and failures will help each of us travel through the world of Social Justice and compassion. His words may help you discover your calling or understand your suffering. Jim will help you stand courageously as a warrior and guardian, putting others first without compromising your integrity.

This book will ground you in life and allow you to live in the faith to which you are called. It is a guide that will encourage everyone from police officers to pastors, perpetrators to professionals, and non-Christians to mature followers of Christ.

1

Jim's real-life stories will keep you engaged. For those that don't like to read that much, the short bursts of challenging content will start your day in the right direction and keep you moving forward in the priorities of life that really matter.

One of the biggest mistakes we can make in looking at either a police officer or a pastor is seeing them or treating them differently because of their God-given authority, making it an "us and them" interaction. Police and pastors are people set apart for a greater purpose, but they are us, and we are them. The best news in this book is that we are all set apart for this greater purpose if we will only accept the training and hit the streets. In a world of chaos, with its lack of civility, its violence and brutality, and the absence of something and someone to believe in, may I suggest we follow the words of wisdom from Jim: "He's One of Us."

Chaplain Bob Fesmire,
Phoenix Police Department

About the Title

Choosing the title for this book was not overly difficult for me. It contains four words that have become a driving force in my life. They are four words that were said about me. However, I confess, they were never said to me. The phrase, "He's one of us" was written on a tiny piece of paper in a cartoon drawn by my partner in 2003. He spent about five minutes sketching this cartoon while we sat next to one another during a squad briefing. I didn't even know he was artistic. But when he handed me the small piece of paper, I was impressed by his talent.

He drew a police car approaching a neighborhood intersection in Phoenix. The window was rolled halfway down, and two people were depicted walking in the same direction as the squad car. At the corner drawn in the cartoon, there lived a man known on the streets as Pablo. His real name was Paul, and I got to know Paul very well. Almost daily, I would cruise down his street to see what was going on in his neighborhood.

Paul was a crack addict but a very nice man. At the time, he was in his mid to late '50s, but due to his lifestyle, he looked as though he could be seventy years old. The prostitutes in that area gravitated around the little house Paul was renting. He provided an opportunity for the girls to get off the streets, have a meal, and even shower if they wanted to. Paul used to introduce me to the prostitutes and tell them I was safe to talk to. What was it about me that made this crack addict feel comfortable enough to endorse me as a good man to others? Maybe it was because I took the time to hear their stories, let them hug me, and call me "Jim" when they saw me approaching. So, looking at the cartoon, I knew the two people walking next to the squad car were Paul and one of the many prostitutes who hung around the neighborhood.

I had to arrest a few people I had come to know in the neighborhood from time to time. But they understood their crimes to be their fault and respected that I did my job with professionalism and fairness. And though I was impressed with my partner's sketch talent, it was the words written in bubbles above their heads that struck close to my heart. Paul, lifting his hand to wave, said "Hey, Ferree." The prostitute walking next to him said, "He's one of us." Looking at that cartoon, I knew my partner understood what mattered most to me as a police officer working in the community. He summed up my simple mission statement in those four words. When a crack addict and a prostitute can look at a police officer in uniform while walking casually down the street without fear and conclude that they consider me as one of them, I have received the highest compliment possible.

I would like to say I started my law enforcement career with this focused commitment, but tragically, that was not the case. In the police academy, due to my ministry background, they called me "Preacher." I didn't take the name as a compliment and felt I needed to prove my strength and valor to be considered one of them. I wanted to show them that I was not some limp noodle passivist thinking I could change the world with goodness and kindness. This was ironic, as none of my peers were police officers yet. So, I remained focused during my time in training.

I made friends with my classmates, but I struggled to balance being an outspoken Christian and my drive to finish in the top five in our class. For the most part, the latter goal was my intent. One of the friends I made was named Brian. He was quiet, a former Marine MP. He was married and had two children. He kept to himself for the most part, and I respected that about him. After we graduated and finished field training, we were sent to the same squad. At that time, the department mandated that all officers ride as partners for officer safety. Nobody on the squad wanted to leave their partner and ride with either of the two new guys, so our boss put us together. Two brand new police officers in a car together. What could possibly go wrong?

Well, we handled ourselves just fine, going call to call, talking through our decisions together. It helped not to have senior officers influencing our judgment. Brian usually took the passenger seat and left the driving to me. On slow nights, having a partner is torture if you cannot find something to talk about. Brain didn't talk too much at first, so I did. Being curious, it was not too long into our partnership that I began asking him questions about spiritual things. But Brian made it abundantly clear that he did not want to talk about religion or anything spiritual.

I respected his space and focused on looking for trouble on the streets. We call that OV work or "on view." As the driver, when something did not look right, I would go check it out. Brian could think quickly on his feet and

4

would swiftly process why I turned a corner to investigate something. We had fun and learned together.

However, I noticed something change in Brian over time. He started talking about his marriage falling apart and other difficulties he was facing. He wasn't emotional, and I wasn't really interested in the distracting conversation. I heard a lot about his struggles between vehicle stops and radio calls, but I offered little to no support. After more than a year together, I moved on to another squad. I saw Brian less and less and never took the time to get together with him while off duty. I didn't even call him to check on him.

One day, I got a call that Brian had taken his life. I was numb and confused. I felt guilty for not keeping in touch. Sitting in the back of a briefing room, the weight of the world seemed to be pressing me to the ground. Then, as if in a quiet whisper, I heard this: "You knew. Learn from this. Don't let this happen again." I took it as divine inspiration, as though I heard the voice of God. I promised God that day to keep Brian's life and tragic death in my mind forever. I promised never to overlook another moment when a person is struggling through a crisis, or through life. I changed that day, learning a very difficult lesson about the reasons why God brings people into our lives.

I also learned that everybody experiences a crisis at one time or another in their lives. But we should not wait for a crisis to step in. Instead, we should cultivate relationships so that in moments of crisis, others know that they have someone who will be a first responder in their lives. Everyone needs a reliable friend who can think about and process what is happening to them without getting caught up in their emotion or pain. We must build relationships with people daily, not so that our lives are richer, but so they know that someone will be with them in their moment of trouble.

I understand you may believe that we need things in common to naturally draw us to another. And we do need friends with commonalities in our lives. But if we limit ourselves only to people that we are willing to get close to, we limit our capacity to love others. This is particularly true for those considered unlovable because they more than most need a friend like you in their lives. I see this principle demonstrated daily by men and women in law enforcement by the way they interact with strangers. I respect how they connect, talking with people on the streets. I see officers comfort the hurting and help the helpless. The uniform they wear permits them to help or respond.

I must confess that when I was a pastor, paid to love and provide care for others, I really did not have a love for people. I wasn't patient with difficult people. However, when I became a police officer, that changed. Hearing stories each day of suffering and crisis, I now love the strangers that tell them. I want to help people, to be the one standing by them in their darkest hour. I know I cannot fix their problem or cause their tragic circumstances to subside. But I can be gentle and kind and understanding. I can offer them a perspective if they ask, or I can get them some water or food. I now love people as a police officer, and I understand more about human suffering and what people in crisis need. I want to be there for people.

When people know we care about them, they will permit us to come into their lives in times of crisis. Sometimes, they need company, someone who can just sit with them. Other times, they need someone to ensure that their basic daily needs, like meals, are met. Usually, they need someone with a level head who can think through their predicament and anticipate upcoming needs to minimize the difficulty of the moment. This is the bridge we must be willing to cross with others. Will it hurt? Sometimes, but the more you do it, the less it hurts and the quicker you will bounce back from the consequences of stepping in.

I believe that now, more than ever, this approach is critical for the healing of our communities. I understand why police officers may take an "us versus them" approach. I understand why police officers may not trust citizens and citizens may not trust police officers. I understand why people may not believe their pastor is relevant in our divisive climate, making it difficult for pastors to get close to members of their church. I understand why Democrats and Republicans can no longer agree on anything, and that discussion to defund the police is deepening the animosity between them. I understand the need for cameras on police officers, yet I cannot overlook the inevitable consequence this has of keeping officers from talking to one another between calls.

Do we need to have things in common to get along? I really don't think so. My partner, when he drew that cartoon, summarized in four words what I believe our world needs. If he saw a crack addict, a prostitute, and a police officer together as one, without being tarnished, offended, or disturbed by the actions of the others, then our communities can see a pathway toward healing. You may not have a positive opinion of police officers because a loved one was mistreated by one. But do you understand police officers? Do you know why they chose this career? Do you know what they have seen, the horrors that keep them up all night? Do you know what they did an hour before they took that call and conducted themselves in a manner unbecoming?

Police administrators are continuously looking at ways police can integrate better into communities. But until the communities invite us in, we cannot progress. Church administrators are continuously looking for ways communities can come back to church, hoping to reclaim the church's relevance in society. But people are leaving the church at a staggering rate, many concluding that its message is no longer relevant to their lives.

This has been the motivation behind writing this book. I am certainly not a writer nor a scholar. This book is a by-product of a discipline I have had in my life over the last thirty years. Almost without exception, I sit down with the Bible and a cup of coffee each morning and read through the pages. I look for ways to tell the Bible's stories in a way as if I witnessed them. I ask the questions I would want to ask if I had been there. I try to infuse myself into the text I am reading. Occasionally, I open my computer and write out my thoughts. So, over the last four years, this book contains what I have written about.

This book was not written to police officers, Christian men, or leaders in the marketplace per se. It was written with the average person in mind, just like me. But I believe what I have written on these pages may touch a nerve or ask a question you may have been contemplating. Many of us need to know the things we think about are normal. I like to tell stories to help others relate better. So, after reading this book, I ask you to consider listening to people's stories. Come into their lives and pitch a tent with them.

It is a brilliant strategy, one employed by the Creator of the universe. God did not think it was too much to send His Son into this world and pitch His tent with us. Through Jesus, God understands human suffering. He's one of us.

Introduction

A cop and an optometrist walk into a bar...

Wow, that sounds like the beginning of a weird joke, right? But that's not quite how it happened. Actually, a cop and an optometrist walked onto a mountain, four mountains to be exact. It was October of 2015, and Jim and I were both volunteers for an inaugural community hiking event in Peoria, a suburb northwest of Phoenix with some amazing hiking trails. The Four Peak Challenge is now an annual event sponsored by Copper Hills Church. The Challenge has participants hike four mountain trails, taking a selfie next to a flag at each peak to document their completion. A couple of weeks before the inaugural event, the 100+ volunteers were invited for a practice hike and lunch to orient themselves with the trail they would be serving on or to experience hiking all four peaks. By chance, Jim and I met at the base of Sunrise Mountain. We completed the practice challenge of all four peaks together. Little did I know that this would be a life-changing day for me.

In the Beginning

I was not a churchgoer. But a few months before meeting Jim on the trail, I had started reading the Bible. Copper Hills Church was in our neighborhood, a couple of blocks from our home. My wife Susan wanted to go and check it out. I wanted no part of this. You see, I was fearful that I would be overwhelmed with a feeling of conviction for all the sin in my life. A public display of weeping was not appealing to me. Reluctantly, I agreed to go.

As we walked into the church and sat down, Jim's 'new people' radar went off, and he beelined right for us. He was friendly, inquiring how we had arrived at Copper Hills. Susan was happy that she was meeting someone new so quickly. I just wanted him to go away and to be left alone to sulk. Jim sensed this and directed his questions to Susan. Little did I know that as a police officer and pastor, Jim has a keen sense of people's hearts. Well, I made it through that first service, and I enjoyed it. After attending a few services, I noticed that before and after service, Jim was always talking very intently with people. I found this a bit curious and wondered what they were talking about. The Lord was about to show me.

Back to the Trail

As we began hiking to the first peak, the conversation started friendly enough. Jim asked me where I was from, what I did for a living, and how long Susan and I had been married. He asked me how many kids we had, what their names were, what their interests were, and where had they gone to school. Jim asked what my interests were, what Susan did for a living, and what her interests were. This went on for the first couple of hours of hiking. I found Jim to be very easy to talk to and immediately enjoyed doing so.

But on the trail to the second peak, the questions got tougher. You see, as a cop, Jim is a skilled communicator. When talking to a suspect, he first puts them at ease by interviewing them. He gets a sense of where their heart and mind are. Then, the interrogation begins. Well, for the next four hours, I was his suspect.

Now it is completely out of my nature to share details of my life with family or friends, much less a new acquaintance. But something moved in my mind and heart that day, which I now know was the Holy Spirit, and suddenly I was telling Jim about the deepest, darkest regrets in my life, both present, and past. But the interesting thing is, Jim offered no judgment or advice about what I told him. He just continued asking questions that led me to my own judgment, to my own conclusions on how I should redirect my life. I am convinced that my future changed for the better that day. That day of hiking made me realize that God puts us where we need to be. There are no coincidences in life—it is all His providence. Heady words coming from a pragmatist as Jim likes to call me; a doctor with a science background that likes to always look for a cause, an effect, and a solution to everything.

About this book

Now I must tell you that Jim is extremely humble, and at first, had no desire for me to put this series of devotionals into a book format. Jim wrote these pieces and shared them with a small group of men, his ministry circle. But through my persistent browbeating during our weekend times on the trail, here we are. Believe me, it was no easy feat to get him to agree to this!

You may notice that each devotional starts on an odd-numbered page on the righthand side of the book. As the book's editor, I did this intentionally to leave some white space between pieces. Placing each devotional into book format, I realized this is a workbook of sorts, meant for underlining, highlighting, and writing down your thoughts. When I first read each devotional, it inspired me to think of ways I needed to change. Perhaps you will feel the same.

My Prayer for You

As you read through these devotionals, I would encourage you to go slowly, finding a quiet time and place during your day to do so. I pray that Jim's words will inspire something in you as they did in me. I pray that you study the verses Jim writes about. I pray that you can listen for what the Holy Spirit tells you as you read. I pray that you will be able to discern the lessons from these devotionals as they appear in your day-to-day life. And finally, I pray that you will share this book with others.

May God bless all that further His Kingdom on earth.

Gary Morgan, OD

He's One of Us

He said, "The one who showed him mercy." And Jesus said to him, "You go, and do likewise" (Luke 10:37)

In 1998, when I made the transition from full-time ministry to full-time law enforcement, I knew I would be exposed to some things I had yet to experience. I had committed this transition to the Lord, asking Him to use me in ways I could not be used in full-time ministry. There were some challenges I was not ready for. The first partner I had on the force took his own life in 2002, about a year after we last rode together. I knew his troubles, and I tried to discuss the Lord with him, but sadly he would have no part of it. So, I ignored his struggles because I still had my own agenda. But after his death, I rededicated myself to His agenda.

Shortly after his death, I met a man who introduced himself to me as Pablo. He was in his mid-fifties, tall, thin, dirty, and had only a few teeth. He was addicted to crack cocaine but usually pretty functional. He lived in a small run-down house at the intersection of 3rd Street and Townley in Phoenix. He used to take in prostitutes who needed to shower and rest. He cared about them, and I admired that about him.

I was on patrol at the time, and Pablo lived in my beat area. I got to know him well. We developed a mutually satisfying relationship. He would tell me who was committing crimes, and I would not search and find drugs on him. He was a harmless man with some bad habits, but I could see the good in him despite his lifestyle. After all, that was par in that neighborhood, so if I couldn't like him, I wouldn't like anyone.

Through Pablo, I got to know all the prostitutes in the area. It was funny. They would see the police car coming down the street and start walking the other way. When they heard me call out their name, they turned back, said hello, and always gave me a hug. They all had a story, and I wanted to know how they got to this point in life. They were relatively happy, and I am sure they enjoyed knowing that at least one cop was not out there to harass them.

A new man on our squad was assigned to ride with me. I thought it would be good to show him how I work the area and let him meet some of the people I knew. Pablo and the girls were nice to him. When they hugged me, they wanted to hug him, but he just could not get himself to do it. One day, as we sat in our briefing, he drew a cartoon, which is on page 8 of this book. He was a pretty good artist. When it was finished, he handed it to me.

The cartoon shows a police car pulling up to the intersection of 3rd Street and Townley next to a male and a female. The man is Pablo, and the woman was one of the many prostitutes we knew. In the cartoon, Pablo says, "Hey Ferree," and the prostitute says, "He's one of us." My partner saw something in me that I had not noticed in myself. For a prostitute to say that a police officer is one of them would be an insult to most of us. But I liked it. I believed that was our Christian duty, to go into all the world, and identify with them, so we can introduce them to a Savior. My secular partner saw this in me even before I saw it myself.

Not too long ago Pablo had a major stroke. I received a phone call advising me that he had listed me as his emergency contact. I would become his surrogate decision-maker since he had no living relatives. After one week in an induced coma, the doctors advised me that he had little brain function and that I could give the order to stop saving his life— so I did. They pulled out all the tubes and he passed away three days later. After all the chaos and emotion that was spent in me, the Lord lifted my eyes to the corkboard in our laundry room. Pinned to the board was the cartoon my partner drew fifteen years earlier, "He's one of us." I guess I really was so to Pablo for him to honor me by allowing me to make such a decision on his behalf.

"And the Word became flesh and dwelt among us, and we have seen his glory, glory as of the only Son from the Father, full of grace and truth" (John 1:14). Jesus became one of us. Not only did man get to see all the fullness of God's glory through Him, but He also got to understand us. He learned what living here was like, knowing full well what living in heaven was like. He understood our pain, our struggles. Through it all, He gives this simple command, "Go and do likewise" (Luke 10:37), showing mercy to others. Thank you, Lord, for teaching me what you meant.

Certainties

"And I am sure of this, that he who began a good work in you will bring it to completion at the day of Jesus Christ" (Philippians 1:6)

Benjamin Franklin said, "In this world, nothing can be said to be certain, except death and taxes." While we have all heard this quote, I think Ben left out a third certainty, *grace*. Paul said to the people in the church of Philippi, "I am sure of this, that He who began a good work in you will bring it to completion at the day of Jesus Christ" (Philippians 1:6). What is Paul talking about here? He is referring to salvation. Since the creation of the world, all things given life have a starting point—a beginning. Eternal life with Christ has a starting point—our *acceptance* of God's grace. Once accepted, God begins His work of salvation in us.

Let's break this down a little further. Paul says, "He who began a good work in you." When God begins a work of salvation, He works it through until the end. God completes what He starts. Not only that, but God also perfects His work. So, for you who have accepted His grace, God has begun His work of salvation in you, and He assures you that He will finish the job. Because of this, our salvation is not contingent on our performance; if it were, we would fail. God does this work for us; that is His promise.

However, grace is a tricky thing. For some, grace is easy to accept. They have a natural propensity to believe that they are worthy of salvation. Others like who they are and trust that their performance has merit. So, they see no need for grace. But for most, grace is difficult. They look at their life and feel they have not earned God's grace. Likewise, they cannot rely on His promise because they do not know the Promise Keeper. They cannot accept what they cannot see (see John 20:29). What most fail to realize is that grace is the easiest thing to receive because God promises grace to those who believe in the redemptive work of Jesus Christ. He is our righteousness. He is our hope.

But how can we be sure of this? After all, some people seem to have a harder life than others. Do you feel you are swimming upstream as a Christian, while others sail smoothly with the current? Do you take two steps backward just after using all you can muster to take a step forward, yet watch others move through life with ease? If you are working hard to keep yourself saved, let me offer a word of advice: stop. Instead, although it seems difficult, trust God's Word. Trust in His promise that your salvation is His priority. And trust that He always delivers.

To further this, in verse 7, Paul tells us how we can be sure of God's promise. He says, "you are all partakers with me of grace." God began in you the gift of eternal life out of His abundant grace and your acceptance of it. So now, God works in you daily out of His abundant grace. And God will finish what He began, and what He is still doing, out of His abundant grace.

Now, *faith* is required to believe this because His grace is a promise with an assured outcome, our salvation. Every time you sit in a chair, you practice faith, convinced that the chair will hold your weight, certain of a particular outcome. Do you have faith to accept that grace has been given to you to save you through all eternity? Trust me, your performance will cause you doubts.

But in verse 6, when Paul said, "I am sure of this," do you hear his confidence in God's promise of grace to those who believe? To do so requires one thing: to know with certainty that His grace is available and that you need it —yesterday, today, and tomorrow. And of course, to trust that His grace is available requires faith. After all, Ben also said: "The way to see by faith is to shut the eye of reason."

May He Win When I Lose

"I want you to know, brothers, that what has happened to me has really served to advance the gospel, so that it has become known throughout the whole imperial guard and to all the rest that my imprisonment is for Christ" (Philippians 1:12-13)

Like many, I enjoy watching the Super Bowl and all the celebrating that follows. I have noticed somewhat of a trend in many of the interviews after the game. Through all the excitement and attention, some of the guys will take the time during interviews to say, "First of all, I want to give all the glory to Jesus Christ, my Lord and Savior." But have you ever heard these words from a player being interviewed from the losing team?

Why does this perspective seem to be reserved only for the winners? Their opponents made it to the Big Game, had a great season, played a great game, and lost on a last-minute field goal. Is the glory to God reserved for the highlights or the winners? Can we give Him the glory for our lowlights or the losses? What if an interview with a player from the losing team started with: "First of all, I want to give all the glory to Jesus Christ, my Lord and Savior, for giving me the strength by His grace to endure this humbling loss." Wow, now that would be a powerful testimony to the greatness of God when under tough circumstances.

Paul began his letter to the Philippians through a lens like this. He said, "I want you to know, brothers, that what has happened to me has really served to advance the gospel, so that it has become known throughout the imperial guard and to all the rest that my imprisonment is for Christ" (Philippians 1:12-13). Did you recognize the perspective in Paul's words here? Paul was sent to prison for preaching the gospel because someone else wanted to win by stopping the momentum of the church. Paul's arrest was "for Christ", and for that, He would be given all the glory.

Paul was a Jew, once among the most powerful in Jerusalem, the Pharisees. In sports terms, he was on the best team in the league. But the people he had prayed and served with became the people who wanted him stopped. Think of a professional athlete that is traded to a rival team and speaks disparagingly about his former team. If you are a fan of the previous team, you no longer think much of that player. The 'home team' Pharisees now cited false accusations against him to charge him (Acts 21:27-29). They arrested him; they wanted him dead.

One may say that Paul was fine with this because he wanted to go to Rome; he used his circumstances to his advantage. Using our sports analogy, this would be like the star player on a last-place team getting traded to a first-place team. Rome was the powerful empire in Paul's time, and he hoped the Lord would somehow deliver him there to advance the gospel. Paul's arrest meant that he would now get a free boat ride to Rome.

To be fair, surely Paul wanted to advance the gospel with efficiency and effectiveness, and he saw Rome as the most influential place in the world to do so. However, he probably preferred not to go in shackles. Yet Paul knew how to give the glory to God through his circumstances, not because of them. He was the humble player on the losing team that knew the next season presented a new opportunity.

How do you handle the lowlights? Do you withdraw out of frustration, so nobody knows how you feel? Do you attract an audience to help you grieve? Do you raise your fist at God and question His love?

Moreover, what do you think people expect to hear from you when your circumstances are unpleasant? What do you think advances the gospel with greater conviction, giving God the glory in our victories or giving Him the glory in our defeats?

I once heard it said, "You cannot NOT be an example." So, the next time you encounter a setback or feel defeated, pray this little prayer: May He win when I lose.

Pressing On

"… I press on to make it my own, because Christ Jesus has made me his own" (Philippians 3:12)

As police officers, we have authority vested in us to chase people. Usually, we know why they are running. It may be that the car they are running from is stolen, or that they just left the scene of a crime. Sometimes, a simple traffic stop, such as for running a stop sign, will end in a chase. In that case, the runner knows something that the officer does not, and the runner does not want the officer to find out what that is. However, I am always amazed at how often the pursuing police officer catches the fleeing suspect.

Early in my career, when someone ran from me, I sprinted after them. By the time I caught the suspect, I could barely breathe and had very little fight left in my body. Fortunately, the person I was running after was working just as hard to breathe; I am glad so few criminals work on their cardio. As my career advanced, I learned how to pace my runs. I knew the one I was chasing was sprinting, and I knew how long an out-of-shape criminal could sprint. He would be able to keep up that pace for about one block, and then he would have to slow down. I knew that if I ran at about 70 percent capacity, I could run about ten blocks and still have fight leftover in me for the arrest. The key point here is that when I chase someone, we both have a goal. The criminal is running away from something, while I am running after something.

Perhaps, this is the reason why police officers usually win. It is much easier to run toward a goal than it is to run away from a problem. The Apostle Paul said to the Philippians, "I press on to make it my own, because Christ Jesus has made me His own" (Philippians 3:12). Paul is referring to perfection, knowing that when he attains resurrection from the dead, he will be made perfect. Paul said, "I press on," meaning he chases it down as though he will catch what he is running after. He runs as though he will finish. He is in hot pursuit.

Assuming we are all running, do we find ourselves running after something or running from something? How often does it feel that the thing we are trying to run away from always seems to run faster than us?

I understand that there are some things we must run from, but there are also things that we should run toward. For the latter, if we are going to run, why not run as Paul ran? Run toward a goal, a prize, a promise, or in pursuit of something worth pursuing.

Some might suggest that running in this way seems to be a lot of work. It sure is. But suppose we don't bother to run at all. Well, things giving chase will catch up to us, and things worth pursuing will never be found. Paul understood this.

It always impresses me that a police officer can see a man sprint from a stolen vehicle yet provide a detailed description of the fleeing man. Once arrested, the officer can positively identify the suspect. This is due to the officer's training. You could say that the trials Paul faced—being whipped, stoned, shipwrecked, and imprisoned—were all part of his training, to remain focused on his goal of pressing on.

Personally, my on-the-job chases are exciting. There are plenty of unknowns around the corner, yet with my police training, focus, and communication, I can press on. Conversely, look at Paul's story through the lens of actually being in Paul's place as each event happens. Talk about unknowns around every corner! He did not have the advantages of a modern-day police officer such as a helicopter overhead or radios to warn him of danger around the next corner, yet he pressed on.

On one occasion, I was chasing a car thief after a bail-out in the middle of the night. The helicopter was overhead lighting up the path ahead of me. When I came to the side of a house, the helicopter advised me an infrared heat signature was being detected from next to where I was standing. I was standing next to a garbage can. The car thief was hiding inside the garbage can! Had I not been in pursuit of the man, the power of the helicopter's technology would not have been utilized. The pursuit displays the power that illuminates the prize.

Paul said, "I press on toward the goal for the prize of the upward call of God in Christ Jesus" (Philippians 3:14). So How is God's prize attained? We must press on toward our goal of God's reward in Jesus and our life with Him. If we don't, we miss seeing His power because we avoid the pursuit.

Perhaps it is time to stop running away and start running after. Paul said, "that I may know Him and the power of His resurrection..."

(Philippians 3:10). But remember, this takes training. At first, you might want to sprint, but this will only get you about a block. Pace yourself, staying focused on the prize God has promised you; it is yours. Run after it steadily, and you will discover that the things you are running from will fade away. Press on.

What Difference Does It Make?

"I know that through your prayers and the help of the Spirit of Jesus Christ this will turn out for my deliverance" (Philippians 1:19)

On Sept. 11, 2012, U.S. diplomatic and intelligence facilities were attacked in Benghazi, Libya. U.S. Ambassador Christopher Stevens was one of the casualties when armed militants overwhelmed a security team guarding the facility. Two other state department employees also lost their lives in the attack. A small contingent of armed U.S. personnel came to the compound in an attempt to protect the Ambassador, but it was too late. The facility was fully engulfed in flames, and the Ambassador was dead in the burning building. The small team took positions on the roof of one of the buildings and fought off surges of militants into the morning. Two more Americans were killed in the hours-long gun battle. Numerous requests were made for reinforcements, but the State Department refused to send ground or air forces to assist.

America's presence in Libya was questionable, and a sizable U.S. counterassault could have led to a more significant conflict and raised concerns that the area was unstable. The assault in Benghazi caused Congress to open an investigation as to the reasons for the failure to provide support for Americans under attack, especially a U.S. ambassador in a foreign country. Secretary of State Hillary Clinton was asked to testify about what she knew, when she knew it, and what decisions she made during the attack.

During Secretary Clinton's testimony, questions arose as to whether the attack in Benghazi was considered to be an act of terrorism. To this, the Secretary answered, "What difference, at this point, does it make?" Her response sparked outrage from some, claiming the Secretary was indifferent toward the loss of these four Americans. To them, her answer to that question made all the difference in the world.

Perhaps Secretary Clinton believed that an attack is an attack, whatever the reason for the attack may be. So, in her defense, her statement is understandable. However, others believe that any attack of an American on foreign soil requires an explanation as to the motive of the attackers. To them, the answer is vital.

23

My imagination sometimes takes me in a different direction. When I reflect on this incident and the response given by the Secretary of State, I am angered that anyone could be so apathetic when lives are at stake and lost. However, as a police officer, I must confess that I have found myself asking the same question under similar circumstances. As I see lives lost, I wonder what difference prayer would have made.

Sometimes, I doubt whether prayers matter. I imagine a committee in heaven (though I think committees will be banned there because they are almost always useless) going over the events of my lifetime, and hearing the question, "Did you even bother to pray?" If I were honest, I would probably say that I did not think praying would have made a difference in the outcome. But I would be wrong.

Paul understood the power of prayer and associated it with the power of the Holy Spirit when he said to the Christians in Philippi, "I know that through your prayers and the help of the Spirit of Jesus Christ this will turn out for my deliverance" (Philippians 1:19). Paul had confidence in prayer and in the Holy Spirit, both powerful forces at work in the affairs of man. The power of the Holy Spirit is indisputable. Can you imagine wondering if the Holy Spirit can make a difference? No, we do not doubt it. Likewise, Paul puts the power of prayer in equal standing with the power of the Holy Spirit. Paul sees the two working together. People pray, and the Spirit helps.

Perhaps the skeptic would say that the Spirit does not need my prayers to do what He wants to do. It seems appropriate to ask how a skeptic would know? Jesus said He doesn't even speak unless His Father gives Him the words (John 12:49). Jesus valued the power of prayer to the point where He heard the voice of His Father and offered nothing but His words. Paul knew prayer complements the power of the Spirit, and that we can directly ask God to grant courage to the persecuted, strength to the weak, help to the hopeless, and sight to the blind.

So, what difference does prayer make? It makes every difference! Paul said "Don't worry about anything, instead pray about everything. Tell God what you need and thank Him for all He has done" (Philippians 4:6 NLT). What would be different in our lives if we were to pray? I would prefer not to have to find out in a committee.

Knowing Who You Are

"The Lord is with you, O mighty man of valor" (Judges 6:11-12)

What makes a man a mighty man? What are the distinctive characteristics of a man of valor? Who comes to mind when you think of this term in our modern society? Do some military generals come to mind, perhaps some who led a great campaign with "shock and awe"? What about some of the great stories about Navy Seals, as depicted in movies like "Lone Survivor" or "13 hours"? We tend to think of acts of bravery on the battlefield and sacrifices beyond the call of duty.

But it is unlikely that Desmond Doss, the World War II medic who refused to carry a weapon in combat comes to mind. He received the Medal of Honor from President Truman for his valor on the battlefield, rescuing over seventy soldiers injured on a cliff, known as Hacksaw Ridge, in Okinawa. He volunteered to serve his country, received harsh treatment by fellow soldiers in training, and had to plead his case before a general for the right to go on to the battlefield unarmed.

Doss was recognized for his bravery based on his many sacrifices for the sake of his fellow soldiers and his country. The enemy pressed him on that ridge, but so were other U.S. soldiers in danger. He could have made it down a cargo net to safety many times, but he stayed, asking God to give him the strength to find one more injured soldier. Nobody saw the valor in Corporal Doss while he was training for this moment, yet his courage on the battlefield went beyond the call of duty. Though nobody else could see it, Doss never doubted who he was. He lived up to who he was.

Desmond Doss reminds me of Gideon. Israel was going through some dark times, always under threat of war from neighboring countries. For seven years, the Midianites (neighbors from the east) had their way with the Israelites. Many of them hid in caves along the mountainside to avoid the oppression of the Midianites. The Jewish people planted crops that their enemy devoured. The 'hand of Midian' was destroying the land given to God's people as a promise because Israel failed to finish their job of clearing out the tribes that remained in the land. As a result, they were living in a constant state of threat and worry.

During this time, God still pitied the Israelites and called on judges to save the people. Maybe some were chosen because of their proven capacity as warriors. That was not the case for Gideon. He feared the Midianites, and when the Lord called him, "Gideon was beating out wheat in a winepress to hide it from the Midianites." But then, Gideon heard the call straight from the top and personally. The Lord appeared to Gideon in human form, sat down by a tree, and said to Gideon, "The Lord is with you, O mighty man of valor" (Judges 6:11-12).

Gideon received a medal of valor while he hid from his enemy. He was unproven and untested, yet he was also undefeated. You see, Gideon did not know his identity yet. He was nobody's hero, and there were no stories told of his life and achievements. I too have been in that position. As a young man, I didn't have a sense of purpose in my life. I was selfish, self-destructive, and did not care. I lived for myself, but it seemed more like I was dying by myself. I did not know who I was.

Then I met the Lord. At first, I was scared. I had no idea why He would want me, or what His intentions were for me. He began to tell me something I had never known. He said I have value because He had given it to me. He told me I am deeply loved, fully pleasing, totally forgiven, accepted, and complete in Him. I finally understood that my identity is not dependent on my performance, nor my accomplishments. I now knew that I have worth because He had given me life. He made me a man of valor, a mighty man.

If you know the story, Gideon was not immediately convinced. Neither was I. I needed some time, and I needed some evidence. After a few more months of living like a failure instead of a warrior, I took a look in the mirror. I said something like this: "I know you love me, but my life does not reflect your love. I know you are my Savior, and I have nowhere else I would rather be than with you." Something was different after that. As men, it is hard for us to accept unmerited gifts. But after that confession into the mirror, I realized that I just needed to acknowledge who I was. He had been telling me all along. I now know who I am. Do you know who you are?

Qualified

(May you), "being strengthened with all power, according to His glorious might, for all endurance and patience with joy, giving thanks to the Father, *who has qualified you* to share in the inheritance of the saints in light" (Colossians 1:11-12)

Recently, while at one of the police precincts, I met a young man who had arranged a ride-along with a police officer. Curious about him, I struck up a conversation and asked him why he wanted to be a police officer. He said his undergraduate degree was in Criminal Justice, and he had just finished his master's degree in Emergency Management. He was particularly interested in managing major incidents, like terrorist attacks. It was evident that he had no interest in the daily grind of being a uniformed patrol officer, the requisite starting point for all who join the department.

Frankly, he was overweight, out of shape, and struggled to maintain eye contact while in conversation. He had difficulty finding words to describe himself but wanted to make the point that he believed his education would be beneficial to our department. In my mind, I concluded that he would never qualify to be a police officer because he would not pass the physical fitness test. Then he said to me, "I have been trying to get a job since graduating, but nobody seems to be impressed with my qualifications." I almost fell to the ground. My first thought was that anyone who has done this job knows our credentials when starting pale in comparison to the credentials we establish while on the job.

Anyone aspiring to be a police officer starts at the bottom when qualifying. The first stage is a written exam, pass or fail. Those who pass the written test are invited to fitness testing. Applicants who make it this far are given a background packet. Once submitted, an investigator scrutinizes the applicant's life. Former employers, friends, and family are interviewed, and every transgression ever committed is considered for disqualification. If the background check is passed, applicants are sent to the police academy, a para-military environment designed to provide a foundational education. Continuous evaluations of physical and psychological fitness, as well as overall aptitude, must be passed to graduate and be commissioned as a police officer.

Once hired by a department, a candidate's first year is spent on probation under the guidance of a Field Training Officer. Street skills are evaluated, and some don't make it. After field training, the officer is solo-capable, meaning he or she is allowed to respond to calls and make decisions. This level of freedom is needed to further test the officer's thought process, work ethic, and determination. After so much scrutiny, most officers enjoy this stage. However, a rookie officer is not considered qualified until probation is completed. Clearly, the qualification process is long and arduous by necessity. And so is the process to share in the work of the Lord.

Have you ever considered what qualifies us to share in the work of the Lord? Do you see yourself as qualified to do the work of the Lord? Do you think the work of the Lord is best in the hands of others? Are there areas in your life that you have determined to be disqualifiers for Kingdom work? Too many stand idle because they believe they are not qualified to share the Gospel and advance the Kingdom. If this describes you, I wonder, have you disqualified yourself or has the Lord?

Paul states that the Father has qualified all of His children to share in Kingdom work. It is as though the Lord Jesus Christ went through the testing process for us and passed at every stage. We have been given a badge, commissioning us for this work. The Greek word Paul uses here, *hikanoó*, means to make sufficient, equipped with the adequate power to perform duties. Our job credentials are the completed work of Jesus Christ and the continuous work of the Holy Spirit who empowers us to advance the Kingdom.

We do not bring our qualifications to Him—He brings them to us. How many times must He remind us that He has given us everything we need for life and godliness? How many times must He tell us that we, though mere jars of clay, are ambassadors on behalf of our King? By His grace, He has called us, delivered us, transformed us, and strengthened us to carry out the Great Commission.

I carry a badge that is a reminder that I am a police officer. Next to the badge is my commission card with the chief's signature on it. The badge is not the credential I need. The commission card gives me the authority to carry out my duties as a police officer. You have been commissioned by the Chief to carry out assigned duties on His behalf. If in doubt, just open your Bible and read your commission card. He recruited you to join the force and to share in the inheritance of the saints. You are qualified for the work.

Focus on Your Target

"Let each of you look not only to his own interests, but also to the interests of others" (Philippians 2:4)

All of us have used binoculars to gain a closer look at an object. Most hunters mount a scope on top of a rifle to help them zero in on a target. When conducting surveillance on a suspect, this tool is an invaluable resource since it allows an officer to focus in from a great distance to gain an advantage. Some scopes even have night vision and heat-sensing technology to help locate or lock in on a target. But scopes require adjustment; they must be focused on the target to be clear.

I recall sitting down the street watching a car thief in front of his house talking to his two sons in the front yard. We were coordinating plans to send in a team to have him arrested, and I was asked to watch and gather any intelligence for the arresting officers. Just before the team's arrival, I saw one of the boys climb into the back of a stolen truck and pick up a gun. He was looking at it with curiosity. Naturally, I was on high alert. I needed to try to determine if the gun was real or fake. After all, even a car thief should have enough sense not to let his child play with a handgun. But the gun looked real. Nothing about it looked like a toy. I radioed the arrest team to stand by and focused in on the gun. I then saw the boy eject a magazine from the gun. It looked too thin, in my opinion, to hold actual bullets (I was sweating bullets). Then the boy pointed the gun in my direction. Now I could see that the barrel looked too narrow to be a real handgun.

Before I said a word on the radio, I wanted to be sure. I kept making small adjustments to my scope for the clearest picture I could get. After a few minutes of watching, I told the arrest team what I was seeing—that the boy was playing with a gun that was not real. I informed the team I was certain, yet I was over one hundred yards away from the boy and basing my conclusion on what I could see through my scope. If I was wrong, the police officers coming in to arrest the man would be placed in grave danger since the boy would be armed, and an officer or the boy would likely get hurt. Cops rarely have the advantage of sustained focus on an object before making a decision. In this case, they had to rely on my word. Without it, if the boy raised the gun, he would be shot.

Shortly after that, the team entered to make the arrest. One officer focused on the boy while the others arrested the man. The boy inadvertently pointed the gun at the officer as he was handing it over. Under any other circumstance, this would have likely led to a shooting. In this instance, the officer trusted my observation and did not react in self-defense. As I pulled up to the house, the officers all expressed their gratitude to me for making sure the gun was not real before they arrived. Without that knowledge, it would have been a terrible situation for the officers to be in. The young boy, appearing to be protecting his father, would have been fired on. The scope stopped that.

The word 'scope' is derived from the Greek word, *skopeo,* meaning to pay close attention to or regard attentively. It implies focus, directed attention, and contemplation. In the Bible, this word is used six times, once by Christ and five times by the apostle Paul. Paul uses *skopeo* to the Philippian Christians when he says, "Let each of you look not only to his own interests, but also to the interests of others" (Philippians 2:4). In other words, look at others as though you are using a scope to do so. Focus on them and their needs, paying close attention to recognize those needs. Contemplate what you see. Direct your attention to the specifics, and then act on them. Sadly, the needs of others often go unnoticed. Today, focus on your target.

The Presence of the Lord

"I am the commander of the army of the LORD. Now I have come" (Joshua 5:14)

I believe the Old Testament gives us some examples of the Pre-Incarnate Christ coming to earth as a man; however, I am not too sure of His body composition. It is possible that at times He only looked human but was not made up of the same DNA as a human. It probably doesn't matter much, although my opinion is that Christ encountered man on this earth before His Incarnation. Did He just appear? Probably. Maybe He took on a human form so man would not be so terribly frightened when He spoke to them. Maybe He took whatever form He wanted to get His message across to His intended audience.

However, I also believe Christ spoke to Moses in Exodus 3:2-6. At the burning bush, Moses said an "angel of the Lord appeared to him." What else could He say? That the Pre-Incarnation of Christ appeared to Him? That would not make any sense. A holy God would send a representative to man on earth to speak His words. It seems to me that this responsibility fell on Christ. Even when the Incarnate Christ walked among men, He made it clear that He only spoke the words His Father gave Him. So, it is not a stretch to conclude that our Heavenly Father would send a representative (Christ) to speak to man in the Old Testament.

I think Moses encountered Christ because he was told to take off his sandals, for Moses was in the presence of God. In the book of Revelation, the apostle John fell to his face before an angel and was admonished by the angel not to worship him, for he was a mere servant. Worship is reserved for God alone. In the case of Moses, the "angel of the Lord" (the Pre-Incarnate Christ) amid the burning bush called for worship.

It is likely that Joshua also encountered Christ as he entered the Promised Land. After the people crossed the Jordan River, they camped outside of Jericho, needing some time to heal from their mass circumcision ceremony. The people then celebrated their first Passover in the promised land. Joshua was ready to take the land, looking at Jericho, probably trying to come up with a strategy when he saw a man standing before him with his sword drawn. Naturally, Joshua was curious as to the man's intentions, "Are you for us, or for our adversaries?" (Joshua 5:13). The man said, "No, but I am the commander of the army of the Lord. Now I have come" (v.14).

Joshua knew he was in the presence of God. He fell on his face to worship. He was not stopped from doing so because it was an appropriate response, and Joshua asked what God would want of His servant. God's representative (Christ) said, "Take off your sandals from your feet, for the place where you are standing is holy" (v. 15). What made this land holy? I believe the presence of the Lord did. It was customary to take off one's shoes when entering the home of a host. It was a sign of respect for the host. Just as the Pre-Incarnate Christ had Moses take his sandals off, Joshua was also commanded to do the same.

In ancient culture, the feet carried a great deal of symbolism. One must have authority over another for the right to have them unstrap their sandals. For example, it was the responsibility of the host's servants to do so for his guests. Christ stood before Joshua and ordered him to remove his sandals, an appropriate demand under the circumstances.

This same Christ would one day take on the form of a helpless child, dependent on His mother for the most basic of needs. He would grow up like any other ordinary man, and He would come to know of the struggles humanity battles on earth. He would distance himself from equality with the Almighty and take on the form of a servant. He would understand us, have compassion on us, and bow like a servant to us. Before His death, He would unstrap the sandals of His disciples and wash their feet. What an image to consider. They once removed their sandals in His presence; now He bowed before them, removed their sandals for them, and served them. What a God we serve.

BOLO

"Be watchful, stand firm in the faith, act like men, be strong" (1 Corinthians 16:13)

BOLO stands for "Be On the Look-Out." Police send out a BOLO to other officers on the street when they need assistance with an investigation such as in locating a person or a car. A BOLO provides minimal but specific information that allows officers to focus some of their attention on assisting. It usually takes only a short time after issuing a BOLO for someone to locate that person or car.

I recall an incident when a squadmate responded to a call of a stolen vehicle. The victim had started his truck, which was parked in his driveway, to warm it up before heading to work. Another truck pulled up, and the passenger got out and stole the man's truck. He watched as both trucks left his neighborhood while he called 9-1-1. The first officer on the scene immediately got a description of both vehicles and stated the direction they were last seen headed. Other officers took positions (called Bull's Eye's) while the officer on the scene put out a BOLO.

I had just pulled into a gas station about three miles from where the truck was stolen when I heard the BOLO. A few seconds later, I saw two trucks make a turn in tandem. The trucks matched the information from the BOLO. I advised our dispatcher and the other officers that I was following both trucks and requested assistance. Both men were caught, and both trucks were recovered (the thief's vehicle was stolen as well). The first officer on the scene did a great job of quickly putting out the BOLO, which significantly increased our chances of catching these guys.

In 1 Corinthians 16:13, the apostle Paul puts out a BOLO for his readers. "Be watchful, stand firm in the faith, act like men, be strong." What does Paul mean when he says, "Be watchful"? The cop in me wants a description: What am I looking for? Should I be on guard, as though I must be prepared to deal with a threat? Should I be anticipating something dangerous? However, the theology student in me knows what Paul's BOLO means. He is telling us to provide our undivided attention to be against anything that can distract us and cause us to drift from our faith.

Paul knew that the trappings of this world cause us to forget what we are about.

So, what can distract us? Can pride distract us? Can wealth distract us? Can popularity distract us? Can our spouse, our children, or our job distract us? Yes, anything can cause a distraction, even good things. Should we abandon everything because of all the threats posed? No! The meaning of Paul's statement is to be vigilant, committed, and strong, and to do everything with integrity. In other words, life is all about options; weigh them carefully.

Recently, I read an article stating that the average American makes about 35,000 conscious decisions every day. Paul reminds us not to let even one of those choices distract us from our faith. Is this possible for you? I say that it is. Although awkward at first, with practice, the right decisions become more instinctive. And right decisions are the cornerstone of our humility, enhancing our ability to serve others.

Paul said to "act like men." What does it mean to act like a man? Is Paul suggesting men show their masculinity? Chivalry comes to my mind, but few know what this means. A knight was called chivalric if he possessed qualities like courage and honor. But a knight was also expected always to be ready to help the weak. Such attributes described the ideal man, and any who aspired to be a knight would consistently demonstrate these qualities. However, these qualities in our modern culture are sometimes used to describe a man who is chauvinistic, overly confident, maybe even arrogant. So how can we heed Paul's command?

In today's society, I feel that a mature man looks to the needs of others. This requires him to possess two characteristics: humility and what I like to call margin. First, humility is not just a vertical posture between us and God; it is also a horizontal posture between us and others. Without humility, our attention will continually fall back on ourselves. Second, planning a little unoccupied time into our day allows us to respond to the unexpected, unanticipated, needs of others—margin. If we leave enough time for these needs, we can react when they surface. How many times have you told yourself, "I would, but I don't have time." Consider this: Today, when you leave work if you say you will help someone before you get home, do you think you will? Do you think you will see an opportunity?

I'll bet yes. Most likely, you will laugh because God has a way of providing the right opportunity at just the right time.

Consider Paul's words as a BOLO sent out to all men. Watch, stand firm, and respond to the needs of others. Position yourself to be responsive. In other words, go where there is a need. Be strategic and intentional. Be humble and never be too busy to respond.

No Longer Living Like Sheep, Part One

"For you were straying like sheep, but have now returned to the Shepherd and Overseer of your souls" (I Peter 2:25)

I have always struggled with the metaphor of sheep to describe Christians. Even before I became a follower of Christ, the idea that someone would suggest I should become sheep-like repulsed me. The image I had of sheep was of helpless creatures who lived in fear and were selfish. They could not be taught, they could not be trained, and they could not be friendly. Beginning in 1987, I spent eight months reading through the Bible, so I could reject its claims intellectually. As a skeptic, I tried to find some reason to reject the claims of Christ. But by 1988, I came to accept that Jesus Christ was the only way, that truth was found in everything about Him, and that eternal life was the gift He came to deliver. However, I did not have a high view of Christians (since I saw them as sheep) and refused to identify as one.

Toward the end of that time, every day for a month I came to the side of my bed, knelt down, folded my hands, closed my eyes, paused, and then said, "Not today God." It wasn't Him I was rejecting, but it was a fear of being a sheep. On Feb. 12, 1988, something changed. It was a miserable day for me. As I drove to work, I could see eternity off in the distance—unreachable. I remained focused within my lane, driving slower than normal. I was afraid to die. When I got to work, a Christian co-worker who knew I had been working through the meaning of being a Christian approached me and asked, "What are you waiting for?" I just looked at him with tears streaming down my face and said, "I don't know." He nodded his head and walked away. He was ok with what he saw in me. He did not strike me as a sheep. He was strong and confident, seeming to know the right words to say at the right time.

That night, I did the same thing I had done every night for the past month. As I knelt, I realized something profound; I was a sheep in need of the Rescuer. I was straying, and the Good Shepherd was coming to bring me out of the darkness. He had a place for me, and I no longer needed to fear. I prayed that He would have me, but I also made one request: "Just don't make me weird." While I knew who God was, I was new at this, and to my knowledge, I had never been in His presence before that day. He received me, put me on His shoulder, and carried me to peace and safety.

I did not see fireworks during my prayer, although I thought I would. In a way, the night was like every other night. However, something was different: for the first time in my life, I stopped resisting God. I trusted Him to be the way, the truth, and the life. He gave me emotion, and the mind to contemplate and work through my doubts. I experienced a freedom that I had not known. Reflecting on the freedom He provides; all I want is to be with Him. I want to go where He goes, I want to hear Him, and I want to talk with Him. I want to be like Him.

The Holy Spirit transforms lives. He changes the believer through His power and boldness so that we no longer live with fear as a natural instinct. Paul said to Timothy, "God gave us a spirit not of fear but of power and love and self-control" (II Timothy 1:7). We lay down our lives, our agenda, for the Great Shepherd, not because we must but because we have peace in Him. We have learned that it's our plans that make us stray. I profess that those who refuse to lay down their lives for Him still walk like sheep. But that is not what we are called to do.

All who do not know Christ are indeed like sheep because they are straying from the Great Shepherd. But I have discovered that many of these people do not deny Jesus Christ as Lord. Rather, they object to their impression of the church as a gathering of sheep getting brainwashed into obedience. If you doubt this perception, ask ten people you know, and most of them would agree. Why do people have this view of the church? This bothers me, and it is something I strive to change.

All of us, at some point in life, have gone astray. Even the disciples of Christ, when they saw Jesus arrested, scattered like sheep: "And Jesus said to them, "You will all fall away, for it is written, 'I will strike the shepherd, and the sheep will be scattered'" (Mark 14:27). However, after Christ's resurrection and return to heaven, something changed. The power of the Holy Spirit transformed the disciples' lives. They were no longer like sheep. They would no longer run. They would boldly proclaim that they were witnesses to the resurrection of their Savior. It would cost most of them their lives.

Fundamentally, I am not a sheep anymore. I have a purpose in my life and a desire to please the Great Shepherd. I know I am now free, and only in Christ is freedom found; something that sheep cannot handle, nor do they want to. But it took the realization that I was a sheep to get here. When He comes to us and places us on His shoulder and brings us back, we are transformed. We no longer stray like sheep. Perhaps it is time for a new metaphor to describe who we are now.

No Longer Living Like Sheep, Part Two

"When he saw the crowds, he had compassion for them, because they were harassed and helpless, like sheep without a shepherd" (Matthew 9:36)

Police culture views society as sheep merrily going through life trying to enjoy the green pastures. Generally, police officers reject the notion that they are one of the sheep. Among the sheep, predators are lurking, hoping to take advantage of the vulnerable. In my unique role on the force as a surveillance detective, I see crimes happen: daily carjackings, armed robberies, and gang violence, to name a few. I know that the sheep need someone to protect them, and police officers naturally and willingly step into that role.

For police officers to be effective, they must be able to distinguish the predator from the prey. With time and experience, they develop an almost instinctive internal mechanism that triggers an immediate response toward a threat, with little regard for their self-preservation. Maybe this is because they are adrenaline junkies; perhaps some are. However, I believe their response has more to do with their training.

When encountering crime, experienced officers have already rehearsed the scenario in their minds. They have practiced their response in artificial environments so many times that their training and experience take over. They effectively utilize this training to fulfill what they have been called to do. Regardless of the threat, society is confident that the police officer will respond, and do so in an appropriate manner, utilizing the amount of force necessary to handle the threat. Society expects this of them; they assume this kind of response from police, and officers expect this of themselves.

When responding to a call, police officers do not view themselves as prey to the predator. Nor do they see themselves as predators fighting predators. If they did, they would abuse their power and unnecessarily bring force to an encounter, engaging without restraint. Now, as I write this in 2018, all police officers are under fire for highly publicized accounts of the authoritative abuse of a few. Some of these instances carry racial undertones and are politicized. But the media does not report on the tens of thousands of incidents that happen each day where the officers respond in the professional manner I have described.

Of course, some committing crimes will die at the hand of police officers; although officers face deadly encounters, it is not what they want to do but what they are forced to do. Police officers do not begin their shift thinking about killing someone. To be honest, most officers think what we all think when we go to work, "I can't wait to get home." With that said, since 1910, an average of more than 150 police officers have died each year in the line of duty. While doing their job, these officers gave the ultimate sacrifice when called to respond. Sometimes, the wolf chooses to attack the guardian to get to the sheep. Most of society understands that the guardian exists for their welfare, while the wolf must be stopped.

So, if police officers do not view themselves as prey or predators, what do they identify with? A growing metaphor that the law enforcement community relates to is the image of the sheepdog, and what the sheepdog does when sufficiently trained. A sheepdog lives with and among its flock, guarding the sheep against predators. Police patrol areas so that residents can see their presence in the neighborhood, which has a calming effect on most people. Police officers are among us while on duty and off duty. Depending on your occupation, they are your customers, clients, or patients, living ordinary lives in our midst. They shop with us at the grocery store. They dine among us at restaurants. They attend their children's athletic events and school plays. They are in our bowling or golf leagues. They attend church with us.

Now I doubt most Americans view themselves as sheep; it is a bit insulting to be described as such. Even if some have sheep-like tendencies, as in following the crowd or running from danger, most probably feel that they are contributors to society, not just consumers. Yet many in our society view church-going people as sheep being herded and refuse to participate because they reject the notion that they are merely sheep. I outlined this misconception in Part One, and here lies the need for a new metaphor for strong Christians. As a cop, I'm partial to the imagery of the sheepdog, and with a little explanation, perhaps you will be too.

When I'm not working, I am still vigilant, like a sheepdog. I view my relationship with God through the same lens. I am under the care of the

Great Shepherd. I know His voice, and I listen to Him. I know His intention, and I obey Him. I know His face, and I come to Him. I have a purpose and would gladly lay down my own life to do His will. He loves me and cares for me. He provides me all I need and equips me for service. I believe He calls me to guard the ninety-nine when He is out bringing in the lost sheep. In a sense, I am always on duty.

The church needs more sheepdogs—would people have a better view of the church if some of us resembled sheepdogs instead of sheep? I realize there will be some objections to the sheepdog metaphor because of the dog's willingness to fight to defend. But does the sheepdog need to fight to be effective? Not at all. The mere presence of a sheepdog is often enough to turn away a threat. Using sheep as a metaphor creates a word picture describing how Christians are often perceived. However, I think it communicates the wrong image, both to those outside of the church and to us on the inside. While every church is a flock, and indeed some are sheep (children come to mind), I believe many see themselves as having a more profound sense of purpose among the congregation—like sheepdogs instead of sheep.

I wonder if more people would respond to an invitation to follow Christ if they knew He was calling them to be sheepdogs, asking them to join Him in His Great Rescue Mission. A sheepdog's purpose is not self-initiated; it is taught at a very young age. By the time a sheepdog is mature, his pleasure is the pleasure of his master. By the same token, we exist for a reason. The Great Shepherd gives us a purpose to live and work. I would suggest that each of us is called for this purpose—to no longer live like sheep. Perhaps you reject the notion that you are to fall in line and follow instructions. If you knew God does not call us to live as sheep, but as His sheepdogs, would you want to be a part of His plan? Consider the metaphor of the sheepdog and decide if you would gladly lay down your life as a sheep and take up your new identity as a sheepdog.

Freedom

"It is for freedom that Christ has set us free. Stand firm, then, and do not let yourselves be burdened again by a yoke of slavery" (Galatians 5:1 NIV)

I have been working on training Koda, our hundred-pound, one-year-old white lab. I confess I got off to a late start with him. For much of the first year, we have kept him around the house because he shows some aggressive tendencies toward other dogs. Training a dog with bad habits is a challenge. But I realized freeing him from his leash would result in his proper training. We live next to a large neighborhood park, and it does not take much to get him out there. So, I walked him to the park and took off the leash.

He loves playing fetch with tennis balls, so I figured I could keep him distracted pretty easily. When I would see someone coming, I put the leash back on him before he took notice. The more I trained him, the more I tested his boundaries. For the most part, I was impressed. He handled people better than I thought, but sometimes I needed to tell strangers how to approach him, so he would not think 'threat.'

Recently, while taking him to the park, I saw another man playing fetch with his two dogs. I figured we would need to just keep moving and keep our distance. However, the man invited us to join them. Koda seemed okay, so I let him go, and he behaved well. The other dogs did not fear him, so Koda just played fetch with me. We had fun, and I felt we were making decent progress.

But suddenly I spotted another dog arriving at the far end of the park. It was a female German Shepherd, and she was off her leash. I tried to put Koda's leash back on, but it was too late. He spotted her and headed her way. I tried calling out to him, but he was locked-on. The hair on his back was standing up, and I knew this meant trouble.

The owner of the German Shepherd did not seem concerned. She kept her dog off the leash as my dog approached. The German Shepherd was standing on a berm looking toward the park. When Koda got within about forty feet of her, she looked at him, remaining calm and in control. She did not see a threat coming at her. If she sensed it, she did not project it.

Koda just stopped. The hair on his back went down, and he looked at her with respect. By her presence alone, she averted a threat. She was older and wiser than my dog and knew how to avoid conflict. Had they fought, I would have given her the advantage. She was in control of herself and her environment. Impressive! Koda just walked away and stayed on his side of the park, never curious again.

This experience led me to think about sheepdogs and how they stand their ground against threats. They do not want to fight, but they will if they have to. They encounter threats with the confidence that they will win if it comes down to a confrontation. If the threat is a wolf, they convince the wolf that any attack is a losing proposition. I thought about what the German Shepherd taught my dog, that freedom comes at a price. If freedom is abused, it can be lost, and there is nothing in the world worth losing freedom over.

Freedom is tough to teach, as it must be experienced to be understood. Giving others their freedom requires risk because control over them must be relinquished. Jesus took that risk on us because he knew we would not fully understand nor love him without it. He freed us. Paul said to the Christians in the Galatian church, "It is for freedom that Christ has set us free. Stand firm, then, and do not let yourselves be burdened again by a yoke of slavery" (Galatians 5:1). Paul taught the Gentile Christians that they were not bound to Jewish law. But freedom is not a license to live as one wants, rather it is a license to live as one should. Sin no longer binds us; we are released from it for a reason. And while it is foolish to go back to bondage, freedom allows for it.

My dog made a good decision, one that I attempted to prevent him from making. It's not that I tried to keep him from making a bad decision—I tried to keep him from making *any* decision. God finds no pleasure in obedience when disobedience is not an option. Can you imagine the joy of our Father when, as freed people, we offer ourselves as living sacrifices? We are given the freedom to do so.

Be a Servant of Christ—Five I's

"If I were still trying to please man, I would not be a servant of Christ" (Galatians 1:10)

When reading this verse, an obvious question comes to mind: why can't I please people and serve Christ? Of course, I desire to be a servant of Christ, willfully accepting God's Word as truth. I seek His instruction and direction. I hear the Spirit of God speak to my heart and respond to its convictions. I love sharing the gospel with the lost, those seeking to understand something they have been searching for their whole lives. It is a supernatural process when we meet someone and discuss the significance of the ministry, sacrifice, and resurrection of Jesus Christ, and they respond out of deep conviction.

However, I confess, I still want people to accept me—I want to please them. I believe my opportunity to share truth with them is contingent on their interest in having a conversation with me. Because the more people warm up to us, the deeper our discussions can be. That's pretty obvious. But there is a trap we can easily fall into. When our desire to be accepted keeps us from speaking about salvation and trusting the Spirit to convict someone's heart, we have forgotten why we are in relationships with people who do not believe. So, while we start with wanting to be liked, we must remember that we need to get beyond that.

Some suggest it takes time to earn a person's respect to allow a discussion on truth. Many say that their opportunity to share the hope of salvation never comes because they never feel confident in their message. But the message of the gospel should be at the top of our minds in every relationship we have. We should unfold that message of hope and peace more and more as a person develops a deeper trust in us. While this may sound difficult, it really isn't. So how do we do this?

To begin, initiate a general discussion about life. What are their interests? Most people enjoy talking about themselves; learn to enjoy listening. While doing so, learn to take an inventory of others' interests, joys, fears, and doubts. Sometimes, you quickly discover what matters most to others, while other times it requires some patience and intentionality. Now, meet them where they are—invest in them with truth.

Truth is God's gift to mankind. He has revealed Himself to us; the Word became flesh and dwelt among us (John 1:14). Though God gives us this wonderful gift, it was never intended to be kept to ourselves. Consider truth as His investment in us to be shared with others. Take a bold risk to let others know that you can relate to their hopes and fears. By investing in others, you set the stage to inspire them with the very truth (His Word) in which you have invested. For example, if you tell someone that God loves him, it is a true statement, but it needs more. Instead, say, "God loves you, and He has a plan for you. He initiates a relationship because He wants to be with you." This is an example of inspiring others after investing truth in them. At this point, most people stop and feel very good about how the conversation went. However, you are not finished. To continue this conversation, invite them to spend more time in the future with you, perhaps a lunch, or a hike, or attending an event. Now, I just listed a simple way to leverage every conversation. An easy way to remember this is what I like to call the Five I's: Initiate, Inventory, Invest, Inspire, Invite. Go back and reread this paragraph. Did you catch those Five I's?

Sincerity is crucial when implementing the Five I's. This technique is not for small talk; most people can sense insincerity. If we do not desire their relationship, our words may sound harsh, and our approach could come across as indifference. Likewise, if a person we engage with tells us something important, we should not seize on that information immediately. We should not offer advice quickly, nor should we offer quick advice. Those who offer advice quickly will usually find that the depth of conversation comes to an abrupt end. Those who offer quick advice either lack empathy or time.

Consider the story of Jesus and the woman at the well in John 4:1-42. Jesus *initiated* the conversation. He had an agenda even before He said a word to her. From His first words, He knew where He was going with the conversation. She revealed her bias to Jesus, opening up about some significant religious differences. When He saw that she was willing to engage, he strategically provoked her. Jesus said to her, "Go, call your husband, and come here" (v. 16).

In today's society, touching a nerve that might make someone feel bad about themselves may be considered provocative. We try to avoid these awkward moments in our conversations. But Jesus mastered the art of taking *inventory* and allowed the details to come out. The woman said to Him, "I have no husband" (v. 17). Jesus took her honest vulnerability and brought the conversation deeper. She soon realized that she was standing at the well in the presence of a prophet from God. She would later discover that this prophet provides a spring of water welling up to eternal life to all that come for Him.

Jesus knew she did not have a husband, yet He gave her that instruction. She had a live-in boyfriend and five former husbands. Jesus was beckoning this woman to open her heart to him. Had she wanted, she could have let Jesus think she was married. She, of course, did not know Jesus knew otherwise. He was a stranger and did not need to know the dirty details. But Jesus understood the hearts of the people He encountered and knew her heart was seeking something more. He told the woman that He is the living water; He *invested* in her with truth. Then He *inspired* her by telling her that anyone who seeks this water will never thirst again. At this point, the woman rushed back to the village she had come from, but she was so excited that she left her jar. Jesus saw this as an opportunity to see her again. When she returned, she brought the people from her city. Notice how this second conversation (v.39-42) had a greater impact than the first. That is why we must find some way to *invite* others to another encounter, whether formal or informal.

Jesus came to the well in Samaria as a servant. Today we have many variants of the well; Starbucks, the office water cooler, or the community mailbox are a few examples. Now, some who come to the well have no interest in speaking with strangers. They reject invitations for conversation and relationship. However, others come to the well at a particular time of day because they will likely see folks they know who come at that time. People who time their visit like this seek meaningful conversation and relationship. If you are someone who times your visits, are you hoping to be liked so you fit in, or are you hoping to be liked so that you can be a servant of Christ through your life to them?

What Enslaves Us?

"For whatever overcomes a person, to that he is enslaved" (II Peter 2:19b)

Sadly, I have come to understand the perils of addiction. I have come to this understanding through hundreds of interviews with career criminals during my years as a detective. At one point in my career, I was assigned to the Repeat Offender Program. The program was designed to handpick certain cases involving repeat offenders for enhanced sentencing. We worked closely with select attorneys, submitting new cases for prosecution. My colleagues and I interviewed repeat offenders who were caught in a serious felony crime. We would work the case, fill in the gaps, and assure that all matters were handled in a timely fashion so that the offender's case did not slip through the cracks.

Once a criminal was labeled a repeat offender, the justice system would apply all of its force to ensure enhanced sentencing. A repeat offender was one who already had at least two prior felony convictions, had violated probation or parole after a prior conviction, had no stable living conditions (like a permanent home, or a family to care for), was unable to sustain steady employment, and showed evidence of drug addiction that lead to re-offending. Studies show that a true repeat offender re-offends approximately every seventy-two hours. Our interviews were designed to determine if the criminal qualified for that distinction.

While working in the program, I developed a loose script on how I would speak to re-offenders. As I covered the entire city, it would usually take about an hour from when I was called to make it to the station where they were detained. By then, they had cooled down and had time to think about their predicament. Frequently, as I entered the interview room, they would ask what my job was. I would never tell them I was working for the Repeat Offender Program. Criminals feared the label and knew how the system worked against repeat offenders.

I would start by stating that I was glad nobody was hurt and then say something like, "I know you would never want to hurt anyone." This statement humanized the offender. Then I would tell him I was not there to chastise him for what he had done, but that I wanted to understand why he commits crime. For whatever reason, this approach seemed to open up these guys. They seemed to conclude that someone would finally listen to them. And, they would talk about everything, including the crime they had committed that got them arrested.

I would explain to them about calculated risk, that we all have within us the ability to consider the consequences of our actions to the extent that criminals will even know how many years a particular offense will cost them if caught. But true repeat offenders reach a point where they stop calculating this risk. I would ask them, "When did you stop calculating the risk?" Every one of them would look down, nod their head, and reflect for a moment on the question. All of them could point to the time when they stopped caring, and it was always due to drug addiction.

These criminals hated addiction. They hated what it had done to their lives, hated what they missed out on because of their addiction, and hated what they had become. Moments of sobriety were not enough; they described themselves as slaves to the drug with no way out. They became controlled by the substance, and the drugs would overcome them to the point that they no longer had the will to fight it.

Peter said, "For whatever overcomes a person, to that he is enslaved." Whether the issue is laziness, bad habits, sexual sin, drug addiction, or bondage due to false teaching, I have found this to be a universal truth. If you find yourself enslaved to something, look back on your tipping point. You will see it lies where you stopped calculating risk, yielding to what controls you. You hate what it has taken from you, but you let it be taken anyway, not because you want to, but because it has you. So, when you reach a point of inability to do what's right and accept a life controlled by something else, you become a Repeat Offender.

Thank God for His grace that compensates for our failure. Thank God that He understands. God loves you just the way you are and comes to rescue you from the depths of your fall. But He does not save us without working in us as hope is discovered in Christ alone. Peter knew this as well as anyone. Peter understood that the foundation of faith must contain some support posts. These posts help strengthen the foundation by which we stand. Peter lists some of these posts in chapter one: "make every effort to supplement your faith with virtue, and virtue with knowledge, and knowledge with self-control, and self-control with steadfastness, and steadfastness with godliness, and godliness with brotherly affection, and brotherly affection with love" (II Peter 1:5-7).

These faith-foundation posts help us think, feel, and act like Christ, regardless of what we face. They help us navigate through options when faced with challenges. They help us see a path that is liberating. But like the feeling of exhaustion after a long run or workday, sometimes we need something to lean on to support us. Our faith can use some support at times, and Peter suggests we make every effort to surround it with these posts.

Looking back at my time in the Repeat Offender Program, it pains me to see how much even these hardened criminals hated being controlled by drugs. They never were given much support; their friends were never much help to them, and they never had much to motivate them. They were fragile, like a boat without a rudder in heavy seas. Nothing was stable enough to hold onto. Is God's grace a motivation to add virtue to your life, or knowledge, or self-control? If so, build a strong faith foundation that contains support posts so that you never become enslaved to anything that can destroy you.

Can God Work Through Us?

"For we are his workmanship, created in Christ Jesus for good works, which God prepared beforehand, that we should walk in them" (Ephesians 2:10)

God's power

One of the great mysteries of the faith, in my opinion, is whether God limits His power, so as His creation, we can operate on our own. Though God's power creates all things, is His design to have all things ready to function immediately according to his plan? Or does God hold back a bit of his power, allowing His creation to grow organically? If we have free will to accept God, does He energize every believer with the necessary power for spiritual completion? Ultimately, it comes down to whether you believe God can work through His creation, or that God does work through His creation. To say He *can* is obvious, so the prudent question to ask is whether He *does*.

When God created Adam and Eve, He created them in His image. A fundamental characteristic of humans that separates us from the animal world is our ability to think, reason, and respond in a way that God would. Humankind is given communication skills to work together, understand each other, and make decisions. We are given a will and emotion, and both play a crucial role in our decision making. Adam was instructed to work in the garden. This seemingly was not a burden to Adam, possibly because God's power worked through him. After Adam's sin, he was commanded to continue to work the earth, but the work would be laborious and difficult. Did he lose some of God's power in his life? Is that why the work would be hard? Did God withdraw His power from future human beings through Adam?

In Ephesians, Paul writes, "In him we have obtained an inheritance, having been predestined according to the purpose of him who works all things according to the counsel of his will" (1:11). If it's God's will to let mankind have a crack at life without His intervention, then one would interpret this verse to suggest that God created, then stepped back and watched. Further, it would suggest that every once in a while, man gets it right, and when he does, God delivers power to the results. Though it is unlikely to hear someone teach that, we often live as though God's work overlooked us, and we are left to make it through life on our own. We come to dark valleys on the journey through life and cry out to God for His strength because ours is depleted.

But in rereading the verse, notice that Paul says God " "works," the verb work is in the present tense. Paul's point is that God works to cause a particular effect. In other words, God expends energy on both the cause and effect of our circumstances. Whether in times of peace or conflict, God is working toward something He has in mind. Whether in good health or sickness, God is not waiting to see how we respond to Him. He is doing something according to His will.

Our sin

Though it is obvious, God cannot lie or sin. Likewise, it is never God's plan that we sin, and He never causes us to do so. Sin is any action or attitude taken that is independent of God. Because we have a will, we can choose to do things our way, and by our strength. If we decide to live independently from God, He will not compete with us. We can live without His power working through our lives. But man's choice to sin was never part of God's will. Yet beginning with Adam, God's entire creation of mankind has chosen that path.

God works

When Jesus bled and died on the cross, do you think God said, "I hope this works?" I cannot accept the suggestion that God did not know precisely what the effect would be of Christ's sacrifice. Undoubtedly, not a drop of His blood has gone to waste—every drop has had and continues to have its intended effect. God gave Christ's sacrifice sufficient energy to begin working immediately, to operate as He planned. Today, He keeps fine-tuning the results of Christ's sacrifice according to the counsel of His will. This gives us hope. Since God will not waste one drop of blood from His Son, it is poured out on us and for us. Every drop has been accounted for. His sacrifice accomplished its intended purpose in our lives and will continue to do so.

God works harder than we ever can or will. It is in His nature to never stop working all things according to His will. God witnessed His Son's sacrifice on the cross and said, "This will work." Consider the circumstances in your life. Are you trying to take over because you think God expects you to work things out, as though God depended on your effort? Do you sometimes wonder if God even knows what you are going through because you feel He is distant and uninvolved? By the will and emotion He gave us, these questions come up when we put ourselves on the throne of our lives. This is a vulnerable position, right where the enemy wants us. But when we put God on the throne (and willfully keep Him there), His work lightens our burden.

Our circumstances are God's tapestry in our lives to complete something according to His purpose and will. So, consider the question we started with: can God work through us, or does God work through us? While we rightly think God *can* do anything, there is one thing He cannot do. God cannot sin—He cannot do something to harm us purposefully. While you may doubt this statement, consider the question, and ask, *does* God work through us? I believe He does. In fact, I am sure He does. What we perceive as trials in our lives, whether they are financial, occupational, health-related, social, or family problems, these may not be of His making. But God *does* use our circumstances to accomplish His purpose. Let him work.

Champion

"And there came out from the camp of the Philistines a champion named Goliath of Gath, whose height was six cubits and a span" (I Samuel 17:4)

The difference maker

Growing up, I was fortunate to have had the opportunity to play on some championship teams. Although teams may have some star players, all members receive trophies and jackets that distinguish them as champs. All of us were winners. In football, our team had back-to-back undefeated seasons. We became champions, then defended our title to keep the honor. Defined as the winner of first prize, we understand the meaning of what a champion is. The right to be called champion is an earned title.

So, why did the author of 1 Samuel refer to Goliath as a champion? Reading the text, I see no record of previous victories that would define him as a champion. The only combat experience written about Goliath says he lost before even raising his sword. As a soldier, he, and all those he served with had likely been victorious. But all who win in battle can claim that title. Yet, the writer did not articulate Goliath's specific accomplishments to define him as a champion individually.

While in the translation Goliath is called a champion, that is not what the writer of I Samuel is saying about him. In Hebrew, *Ish HaBenayim* means "the space between two armies" or "the man between two." Goliath was the reason why Israel would not fight the Philistines; he was considered the difference maker if the Philistines went to battle. The Philistines were so confident in Goliath that they allowed him to declare that whoever defeats him defeats their entire army, and the Philistines would serve the Israelites if they could beat him.

Another way to look at this is that Goliath's provocation each day against the Israelites served to maintain the peace between the two nations. I realize it is almost impossible to read of Goliath and glean something positive about this giant of a man, but essentially, he stood in the gap between the two forces. The writer's use of *Ish HaBenayim* is meant to distinguish Goliath as a significant player in the conflict between the two nations. Eventually, we would meet a young man named David who would stand in the gap to oppose the "champion."

David listened to the taunts of Goliath and watched the Israelites shrink in fear. King Saul had even promised the man who challenged and defeated Goliath great riches and one of his daughters in marriage, but no one took his offer. Goliath's reputation preceded him as he stood before the Israelites. He was confident that no man would oppose him, and until David arrived, none did. But David saw Goliath's threats as a challenge to the Almighty God and His power. David knew that if a man would just stand and fight to defend the glory of God, Goliath would be defeated.

Stand in the gap

Today, why are men like this so hard to find? Now, I am not referring to a warrior or a fighter, but to those who are willing to stand between two forces and make a difference in the outcome. In modern society, we find ourselves living in a world opposed to the Kingdom of God. We recognize the growing gap that exists between culture and Christianity. Some Christians find it wise to blend the two, so the divide is not recognizable. I do not think this is the solution. Others believe we must fight against cultural trends and take our stand. I don't feel that is wise either.

I believe we need to stand on the front line of the battle, close enough to hear the taunts from those who oppose us. We must maintain a space between the church and culture, recognizing the force behind each. In doing so, we will stand in the gap and keep the peace. We don't have to convince the opposition that we are right, and they are wrong; we just need to accept them as opposition and refuse to give up more ground. If the division gets greater, let it be because the forces of this world step back. Our presence on the front-line ought to demonstrate the glory and power of God, the power He gives us to display His glory.

During the time of Ezekiel, the prophet, the Lord saw that the poor were being oppressed and the people were committing crimes against one another. The Lord said, "And I sought for a man among them who should build up the wall and *stand in the breach* before me for the land, that I should not destroy it, but I found none" (Ezekiel 22:30). As a police officer, I desire to keep the peace. I don't want to bring force against a wrongdoer, but I will if they seek to harm me or another. But I cannot do anything unless I stand in the gap, at the front line between lawbreakers and law-abiding citizens. There is no place I would rather be in my job, in my life, and in my church. Join me, and let's be champions together.

Be Watchful

"Be sober-minded; be watchful. Your adversary the devil prowls around like a roaring lion, seeking someone to devour" (I Peter 5:8)

During most of my law enforcement career, I have worked on a unit assigned to watching criminals commit crimes and have learned a few things about them. It is a unique assignment because most police officers don't observe crime from beginning to end; they respond to a crime in progress or one that has occurred, usually because someone else reports it. Our assignment requires that we are present while the perpetrator commits his crime. When criminals pounce, we are covertly in the area watching them work. Operating in this manner helps us profile the minds of two types of criminals, *prowlers*, and *predators*. We learn why they choose a particular house, car, or person for their crime.

Prowlers

Three elements must be in place to be a victim of a prowler. First, a prowler must be on the prowl—he wants to steal something. Your property is safe if nobody wants to take it. A brand-new set of Ping® golf clubs on the front curb of your house will remain there if nobody with the intent to steal it comes along. Second, a prowler must have an opportunity; he chooses a path of least resistance to get what he wants. He will not pick a house that is well guarded or well-fortified. Open garage doors present easy access for a prowler. If one comes into a neighborhood with every garage door open, he probably will not steal from every house, but choose the garage that yields the maximum gain. Third, a prowler does not want to get caught—he looks for assurance that he can accomplish his goal while remaining undetected. My favorite part of my job is watching these guys look around thinking nobody is watching them.

One of the most interesting aspects of my job is the science of profiling the prowler. For example, watching, over time, one choose his target helps us to learn why he selects a particular home over another. Corner houses with low backyard walls, homes with carports, and homes against an open field with a good view inside are preferred targets. A prowler can hide for hours watching the patterns of a homeowner. He then chooses the best time and access point to break in. By observation, investigators can predict a prowler's behavior and know which ones will find another victim and re-offend.

Predators

With the added dimension of making their crimes personal, predators have the same characteristics as a prowler. Predators take property, sex, or life from their victims. When we encounter predators, our approach is different. We will not allow someone to be victimized by a predator. We will engage, chase, and intercept a predator to protect a victim to the best of our ability. As we do with prowlers, our unit also profiles predators. We see why they choose some targets and not others. For instance, we have followed predators that do 'street jumps' on oblivious people who are looking at or talking on their cell phones. Unfortunately, we cannot stop everything. I recall instances of pursuit where culprits have carjacked a vehicle before we can approach and protect the victim. These occasions bother me and my squadmates but motivate us to learn from them for the future.

The devil

When I read 1 Peter 5:8, I see both a prowler and predator in the devil. However, property is not the devil's interest. He is like a roaring lion looking for someone to devour. I see the same elements in the devil's nature as I do any other prowler or predator. First, he is always on the prowl looking for an opportunity. Second, the devil knows when an opportunity exists to attack. He has studied the terrain, watched his victim, and identified his point of entry or access. He looks for unguarded walls, oblivious bystanders, and unprotected, vulnerable victims. He knows what he wants and can wait for the right time to pounce. Third, the devil does not want to be noticed. He likes to slip in, take what he wants, and slip out. He does not want anyone to know he was in the neighborhood. He hides well until he is ready to devour. If he came in announcing himself and his intentions, people would run. But the devil does not chase. He takes advantage of an unwitting victim.

Metaphorically speaking, sometimes we leave our garage door open for the devil to see. Whether intentional or by mistake, sometimes we are not watching. We make it easy to be assailed. The devil is an opportunist, and Peter tells the reader to "resist him." That's the right advice, but how is this possible if he is hiding? Well, it requires some attention—perhaps there is a science to the victimology of the devil's schemes.

At times, I have let my guard down and created my own vulnerable access points. Like anyone else, I have at times failed to remain watchful, to see the devil's movements through the high brush of life. However, I have discovered that if I stay still, I will notice movement in the bushes. I will hear the sound of the fiend laying low and moving in.

So, be watchful. Secure your home, watch where you are going, listen carefully, and stay on the path God has illuminated for you. The devil might not attack if you remain in the light.

Timing, Character, Response

"At an acceptable time, O God, in the abundance of your steadfast love answer me in your saving faithfulness" (Psalms 69:13)

Are you at peace with God's timing? Give the question some thought. Think about a time or times when you prayed for God to act. How did He respond? Was He ever late? Was He ever early? Did He meet your expectation with an appropriate response? Have you ever shaken your fist at God and told Him He was too late, that He should have been there sooner? When you thought He was late, have you looked back to see that His timing was perfect?

As a police officer, I have previously struggled with the issue of timing. I believed I was called by God to respond to critical incidents, yet so often my response was too late. Well, at least it was in the minds of grieving family members who shouted at me that I was too late. Believe me, there were times when I agreed with them. If only I had been there sooner to provide aid, to call in support, to spot the fleeing suspect vehicle, to save a life. Through much heartache, I needed to resolve the issue of God's timing as a means of self-preservation, at least in my own mind.

During critical incidents, citizens rely on a rapid response from law enforcement personnel to come to the scene, render aid, look for clues, solve the crime, and arrest the perpetrator. To the heartbroken family, this is rarely done fast enough. I learned to understand their frustration. After all, I asked the same of God countless times in my life. I have made that heavenly 9-1-1 call and waited in panic much like a victim's family—as if I were standing at the curb and looking up and down the street waiting for a response. When the response I wanted didn't come, I concluded that God was not given the call to respond. I understand when someone feels like God does not care.

But He does—His timing is perfect. I have peace now, but not because God responds quicker than He used to. If God did for me everything I asked Him to, I would be a god. I have come to have peace because I have developed a trust in Him. He owes no explanation to me when He seems late. It is one of God's great character traits; He is always on time. Sometimes, we walk through dark corridors with only a reflection of light seen up ahead. We must trust the light and continue through our hardship. We pray, "Lord, takes us out of this struggle." Perhaps we should learn to ask Him to take us through it instead

In Psalm 69, David finds himself in one of those places he wishes he was not, "the waters have come up to my neck" (69:1). What do you think David meant when he spoke of waters up to his neck? Has there been a time in your life when you have been in the same place? What happened next? Did the waters quickly recede? Did you call out to Him and get a response? Did you panic or were you at peace? Is it possible to be at peace in a moment like this? At times when a crisis in your life reaches up to your neck, and you are on the verge of panic, there will be some who are standing on a safe platform telling you to relax, to give it to God, to be at peace. It just does not seem to be the best advice at the time, does it?

In Mark chapter 4, Jesus said something similar to His disciples on the boat during the storm. The episode illustrates that they did not trust who He was or what He could do. They observed that Jesus remained calm in the storm while they were panicking. The disciples asked Jesus, "Teacher, do you not care that we are perishing?" (Mark 4:38). But they were not perishing, they just thought they were. They did not see the big picture, and they did not know how the scene would play out. If only we could see how calm God is when we face deep waters.

Can you imagine the confusion of His disciples the day after His death on the cross? They knew He had authority over nature; He had calmed the waters when they thought they would die in a storm at sea. Then they saw Him die on the cross. Wouldn't they wonder why He did not have authority over the Roman government or over the Jews who wanted Him to die? As it turns out, not only did he have power over them, but also over death. God's perfect timing illustrates his patience so that His will be done. God always has a perfect plan, even in the midst of deep waters.

As a police officer, I have come to know the peace in His timing. That is not to say I do not hurt or cry. I still do. I understand the pain one feels when they think God was too late. Many of us have struggled to reconcile how a loving God would allow us to feel such pain. But this pain has a purpose in God's economy. We cannot trust God in deep waters if we never get wet.

Did you ever go to the beach as a child? How did you approach the water? You probably ran from the waves. You walked out as far as the water receded between waves, then as the next wave crashed, you ran, trying to stay ahead of the advancing wall of water. Likewise, we often live in a similar way. We are willing to serve or give as long as we are in control of it. However, we will not discover God's power until we are in a place where God's power is all we can rely on.

Psalm 69 draws attention to God's timing, God's character, and God's response. In the midst of deep water, David acknowledges some essential truths about God. He concedes that God is in control and that He decides when the water recedes. David confirms that God is good and that His love for us motivates him. This also means we are sometimes where He wants us to be, but we don't want to be there. Finally, David acknowledged that God gets the final word. He has an answer and can give it to us if that is what He knows is best.

Do you have the faith to accept God's timing? If He tells you no, or not now, will you endure, confident that He is in control? If He tells you why you are going through adversity, will you remain faithful to Him without questioning His goodness? Are you sure you want to know *why* you are in up to your neck? If you could know everything you will go through for the rest of your life, seeing it all in advance, would you really want to? Do you think you could handle it? You can handle it: trust His timing, trust His character, and trust His response.

Selective Obedience

"Why did you not obey the voice of the Lord?" (I Samuel 15:19)

Saul as king

Samuel was a faithful leader to the Israelites during the time of the Judges. However, the people saw that the surrounding nations had legitimate governments ruled by kings. The Israelites wanted the same and appealed to Samuel to appoint a king for them. The Lord spoke to Samuel and put forth Saul as the first king of Israel. Saul was chosen because the people would accept him as their leader. He was taller than most, and Israel would accept a king measured by such shallow standards. Unfortunately, the people were not the best judge of character.

As king, Saul was responsible for the people of Israel, yet he still relied on Samuel as a prophet to provide instruction from the Lord. Through Samuel, Saul directed the people in battle by the Lord's orders, leading them to defend and claim land. A pretty simple formula, as long as Saul and the people obeyed. Initially, Saul did his job according to the instruction given to him by Samuel. But pride rapidly consumed Saul, compromising his leadership capacity.

The Lord told Samuel to have Saul strike the Amalekites and destroy everything and everyone. Saul responded by bringing a force against the Amalekites but sparing their king and best livestock. Samuel was angry at Saul's disobedience. After all, he had given the people he loved a leader they wanted. The Lord gave Samuel a message for Saul: "Why did you not obey the voice of the Lord?" Saul's response was interesting. He challenged the premise that he was disobedient.

Saul's selective obedience

Saul told Samuel that he did obey the Lord. He fought against the Amalekites, going on the mission the Lord gave him. The king of the Amalekites was captured, and the populace was destroyed. Then he told Samuel that his forces that went into battle took the spoils, claiming the best livestock. Saul stated that his purpose in allowing this was to have the finest animals for sacrifice to the Lord. In doing so, Saul had selected what parts of his mission to carry out.

Such selective obedience is not obedience at all; it is a convenience. Saul was responsible for his people, assuring that they followed the commands the Lord had given him, but he failed. He spared the Amalekite king and made an exception for his army to keep the spoils. Was Saul's motive to seek respect from his men? Was he approached by one of his army officers asking for this compromise? Whatever the reasoning, Saul's failure to obey all the Lord commanded resulted in his rejection by the Lord as king of Israel. Saul was replaced as king by David, a man after God's heart. David was not a perfect man, but he understood the responsibility of accepting the Lord's call and did so with humility.

Our selective obedience

When the Lord gives us instruction, does He ask or tell us to obey? Some suggest that it is the Lord's nature that He would ask, not demand. Perhaps that is true, but would you consider taking a more in-depth look into this? If you have ever heard the quiet whisper of the Lord speak into your heart, and you conclude He has called you somewhere or to something, do you recall it sounding like an order or a suggestion? A suggestion usually implies there is another option. I believe that His message to us is clear and specific—not a suggestion. He speaks into our hearts and convicts us into action.

Saul, however, thought that he knew what was best. I admit that there are many times that I have found myself, like Saul, in a discussion with the Lord, questioning His instruction. When I look back on these times, I realize how ridiculous my reasoning was. Imagine, me trying to tell Him what the conditions are like down here on earth, as though he does not know. Ultimately, I am trying to find excuses to not obey the Lord; I am guilty of selective obedience.

The remedy to our selective obedience is to accept God's call in our lives. The will of the King of Kings is to be followed by those under His authority, responding accordingly and without rationalization. He is clear as to what He expects. He expects us to obey Him, yet He does not make obedience a burden. He wants our obedience to come from a humble heart, dependent on Him for everything. He promised to take care of us. He wants us to embrace His promises by faith. Seek Him first.

If we come to Him, humbled and grateful, He will give us a new heart that desires Him. Once a new heart is firmly established, obedience follows. Do not try to obey in order to be loved by God. This cannot work. Also, don't pick and choose how and what to obey. We cannot arbitrarily decide which of His commands to follow. That behavior would not go over well in our workplace, so why do we think it will go over well with God? Selective obedience is just a convenient way to live for ourselves. To fully accept Him as King, let Him have the final word.

The Finished Product

"Therefore do not be anxious about tomorrow, for tomorrow will be anxious for itself. Sufficient for the day is its own trouble" (Matthew 6:34)

Today is a rehearsal for tomorrow. Think about it. The situations we are dealing with today play a significant role in how we will face tomorrow. Today is so critically important that it will likely shape tomorrow. Tomorrow depends on what we do or how we respond today.

For example, let's say that a husband and wife are arguing and cannot resolve the issue before going to bed. How much of an impact does this have on their attitude toward each other in the morning? Unless there is reconciliation before they go to sleep, their tomorrow will be shaped by the argument that happened the day before. Consider how much more they must overcome if they failed to handle the problem the day before. That is not to say poor decisions cannot be salvaged. However, those poor decisions today have much to say about how tomorrow looks.

The key, of course, is to deal with today without dismissing it until tomorrow. What I see here is that each day brings concerns or troubles that need to be addressed. If not, tomorrow is much more difficult than is necessary. If we push our problems to tomorrow, are we not creating unnecessary anxiety? Procrastination only adds to the stress of getting things done. As I write this, our daughter is about to get married. She is excited about the wedding and planning the details. The list of "to do's" is overwhelming, but the sooner they are completed, the more at peace everyone will feel about the upcoming big day.

You see, today is important because tomorrow is contingent on it. However, we may be thinking that Jesus does not want us to be concerned about tomorrow, as stated in the opening verse. While this is true, today can give us a head start for tomorrow, if we take care of today. Simply put, I believe God cares about the finished product of our lives. He loves to see progress, and he knows that each day's fires act as refining agents that purify our souls. Today may be difficult, but it is in preparation for tomorrow. In the parlance of the United States Navy SEALS, "the only easy day was yesterday." Better yet, today is in preparation for eternity, when we will stand before the Creator as a finished product.

Upon their Exodus from Egypt, the Jews, led by Moses, wandered through the wilderness. Each day had challenges, and each day looked a lot like the previous day. Life must have felt mundane to some, even pointless. And for those who lost sight of where they were going, I am sure they found good reasons to grumble. Recalling the events in the wilderness, Moses said it was the Lord who brought the people out of slavery in Egypt. It was the Lord who led the people through the vast and terrifying wilderness, filled with scorpions and snakes. It was the Lord who brought water out of a flinty rock. It was the Lord who fed the masses daily with manna, a bread created by God, just for them.

While in the wilderness, each day brought its own set of troubles. The Jewish people lost their focus on today, failing to see its purpose. But God was using each day to teach the people His law. They were to speak about it daily, so when they reached the Promised Land, they would know what God expected of them. God was also using each day to show His glory so the people would worship Him and only Him. However, the Jews cared so much about tomorrow, that they failed to live today. Our lesson from this is that we must learn to trust God today, accepting that which He calls on us to handle today, and faithfully honor Him in all we do by finishing today's work.

In those times, God had His purposes for life's trials, just as he does now. But at the time, the Jews rarely understood His reasons, and today, neither do we. In a moment of reflection toward the end of his 40-year journey leading the people through the wilderness, Moses said to the Jews: "that He might humble you and test you, to do you good in the end" (Deuteronomy 8:16b). Likewise, everything we must face today has a purpose for our lives. While Jesus tells us not to be anxious about tomorrow, is it ok to be anxious about today? Well, if the trials we face today are severe, I would imagine that God expects us to have some anxiety about them.

God will not hurt us. He will help us, but we must approach our anxieties from that perspective. God will not waste the lesson He has for us today, nor will he cause us so much grief that we cannot handle it. Too often, we assume our most difficult times in life are the result of a distant God. Just the opposite is true. God is close when we are under fire. He wants us to trust Him. The trial may continue, but only because God has a shape in mind and will use the fire to mold us into His likeness. God has a finished product in mind. Face each day, one day at a time. Learn what each day is teaching us. Do not rush growth, and do not worry. God knows how to get the finished product He is looking for and needs us to get there each day.

Be Like Men

"Stay dressed for action and keep your lamps burning, and *be like men* who are waiting for their master to come home from the wedding feast, so that they may open the door to him at once when he comes and knocks" (Luke 12:35)

I love the imagery here of a gatekeeper waiting in anticipation for the uncertain moment when his king returns from a wedding feast. The gatekeeper does not sit down, take a lunch break, nor call in for his replacement. Instead, he stands in readiness; he wants to be working when his master the king arrives so that he can open the gate for him.

I am a plainclothes detective, and our squad works on the streets all day. If you were to see us, you would not think we were police. We dress to blend into society, going about our business like everyone else. Not long ago, I heard over our scanner that a car thief was running from uniformed officers. Being nearby in the neighborhood, I switched over to that radio frequency and started toward their location. I could hear that the officers were chasing the man on foot. I then saw the officers running toward an elementary school. Suddenly, a man came running out of the south doors of the school, heading toward me. I had not yet said a word on the police radio that I was in the area, so the officers giving chase did not know that I was present.

The young man ran in front of my car with the uniformed officers still some distance back. He obviously was unaware that I was a police officer. Procedurally, I should have stopped my car, exited, and forced him to change course or surrender. But I was not ready to engage the criminal. I keep a tactical vest in my car to put on before I take police action. The vest provides ballistic protection, and it also displays clear markings that I am a police officer. However, this situation came upon me so quickly that I was unable to put on my vest.

He ran into a driveway on the passenger side of my car, so I pulled in behind him to follow. He turned to face me from the right side of my vehicle and began reaching into his waistline. Police officers always watch a suspect's hands and making a move to the waistline is never a good move in front of a cop. Slamming my car into park, I ducked down while opening my car door (anticipating shots to come my way). Drawing my weapon and expecting a gunfight, I looked in his direction as I exited my car and saw that his hand was still on his waistline. He was trying to fool me into thinking he had a gun so I would back off. He was not armed.

Nevertheless, he had the advantage over me because I was unprepared. I did not have my tactical vest on: I had no ballistic protection, I had no identifiable markings showing I was a police officer, and I was in a disadvantaged position. Worse yet, uniformed officers were approaching, and I was the one pointing a gun—they did not know I was in the area. I even failed to announce that I was a police officer! I placed myself at risk because I was unprepared. Fortunately, the responding officers made a quick assessment and concluded I was not a threat to them. Had they turned on me, they would have been justified, and I would have been the one responsible. I got away with one.

You see, I was not ready, and I came into a situation where I should have been. Though counter instinctive, I should have maintained my distance, announced my presence over the radio, and directed the officers to the suspect's location. By engaging the suspect unprepared, I put all the other officers (and myself) in a compromising position. That is eye-opening and sobering, and I am grateful I have the opportunity to still tell about it.

Jesus reminds us to "be like men" who are waiting (and ready) for action. Most of us are not going through life waiting for a car thief to run in front of us. However, we face differing situations. What are the moments that you find yourself passing through? Do you see a friend in need or a stranger in distress? Are you prepared to engage? What if the one coming was the Lord Himself? Would you be ready with a response? Do you live your life in such a way that you anticipate standing in the presence of the Lord at any moment?

Jesus did not mean that only "men" need to be like men, rather all of us (men and women) need to be ready and in a constant state of anticipation. "Men" need to know what to expect, so they know how to be prepared when a situation arises. "Men" need to live in such a way that the mere sight of the Lord coming in their direction gives them joy, not fear. How many opportunities have passed us by because we were not ready when they presented? I know I have missed my share.

What does a state of readiness look like in your life? Are you one of those men? Any close calls to remind you of the need for a state of readiness? Whether a medical condition, a job challenge, or a relationship struggle, stand ready as one holding a burning torch at the gate anticipating the King to come home. Don't let the fire go out. Be prepared, dressed for action. This is life—be like men.

Teaching Freedom

"For freedom Christ has set us free; stand firm therefore, and do not submit again to a yoke of slavery" (Galatians 5:1)

Grace and Freedom

I have discovered that two of the most challenging concepts to teach are grace and freedom. Both of these concepts challenge our pride since both are gifts given despite our efforts. We have a propensity to refuse these gifts as unearned. When we consider grace, we struggle to separate our work from faith. When we discuss freedom, we include some degree of our responsibility for it. So, both gifts are often misunderstood, abused, or disregarded altogether. While we may accept some extent of both, many of us struggle to embrace them as absolutes in our lives. Here is a truth statement worthy of memorizing: Grace is God's love on full display; He gives what we can never attain. Freedom is God's patience on full display; He lets those He loves choose to love Him.

Now, when discussing freedom, someone always warns that we must not overlook sin. Though I agree, constricting freedom to choose to do what is right means preventing people from doing wrong. If that is what God wanted, He never would have placed the tree of the knowledge of good and evil in the garden. You see, there is a difference between obedience by force and obedience by choice. Forced obedience is compliance. Choosing obedience produces worship. When I was a youth pastor in the '90s, I met many teens who had not yet been given the freedom to make choices. I could see a desire in their eyes to be released so they could navigate freely through life. I still see this happening—many Christian teens will notice that friends who do not go to church seem to have more freedom than they do, resulting in rebellion for some. And it is not that the rebellious crave sin; they just desire to be free to choose for themselves. This creates a fine line that parents and youth leaders must walk; worship by compliance is not worship at all, and it leads to sin.

Respecting freedom

As we age and reflect on our freedom, we often realize the dangers we unknowingly faced when we were younger. My two brothers and I are close in age. Growing up, our dad worked for a large building firm. Moving from project to project was expected of him. We did not stay in the same place for very long. Through all the moves, my brothers and I stuck together like friends. At a young age, our mom gave us the freedom to roam. Her only request was that we were home for dinner. Because of our father's job, dinner was at sundown, so even without a watch, we always knew how much time we had until dinner and never missed one.

In the mid- '70s, we lived in Walnut Creek, California. Our home was next to a BART station (Bay Area Rapid Transit). We had BART passes, so we often took trips to unknown destinations— three young boys, free to roam without boundaries. After all, my fifth-grade brother was responsible enough to ensure that my second-grade brother and I remained safe. Today parents will read this and wonder what our mother was thinking; wasn't she worried? Heck, if this were to happen today, my mom and dad might be arrested! Yet through it all, my brothers and I always made it home for dinner. We had respect for our rather large boundaries. As a result, we have some fun stories we tell when we get together; stories that were made because we were free to make them. However, I must confess we did not always make the best choices while we were out and about.

Are we meant to be city dogs or country dogs?

Consider for a moment a dog raised in the city. It is kept indoors with no way out on its own. It looks out the window, watching life pass by. When taken outside, it is put on a leash and led only where its master chooses. City dogs may scratch at the door to go out, but perhaps they are really plotting their escape. And the city dog's master knows it will run if let out on its own, potentially never coming back, so it is never permitted.

Quite the opposite, a dog raised in the country hangs out on the porch. The world is its oyster, with the freedom to come and go as it pleases. It is rarely on a leash and can travel far from home while seeking adventure. Or it can just sleep around the house all day. The country dog understands who its master is, knows when mealtime is, and the link between the two. The country dog is free but always comes back to the porch.

Which of these two dogs describes how you perceive God? Do you think God wants to keep us in the house to make sure we are safe? Do we have to prove ourselves to Him, that we are responsible enough to walk freely? Or do you think God lets us out, leaving an open door to show us the extent of His love and patience? For those who believe the latter, there is no doubt that some will run. But others will stay.

Freedom's demise

In today's society, people tend not to trust freedom. We all want it for ourselves but struggle to accept it as best for everyone, so it is restricted. And when freedom is abused, those that allowed it are often held accountable. Accordingly, those that can limit the freedom of others establish rules out of anxiety—rules they believe are best when followed. Those that make the rules fear what may happen if freedom leads followers astray.

Essentially, rules are made by leaders, including government and church leaders. In the latter case, although many may have good intentions, fear overcomes some and control is established. Many pastors, elders, and church leaders fear what freedom may cause in the church. Is this what we are called to as leaders of the church? What is the gospel without freedom? Christ calls us to freedom: risky for the recipient and the giver.

Christ's freedom

Jesus said, "So if the Son sets you free, you will be free indeed" (John 8:36). So, it is for freedom that Christ has set us free. Subsequently, for those we love most, do we offer them the gift of freedom? Or do we feel it is irresponsible to do so? In other words, do we trust those we love with freedom or worry about the repercussions if they betray that trust? Undoubtedly, we all will find a certain level of discomfort with this topic, some likely more so than others. Now, think about what Jesus went through to provide your freedom—uncomfortable, isn't it?

Why People Lie

"Exhort one another every day, as long as it is called "today," that none of you may be hardened by the deceitfulness of sin" (Hebrews 3:13)

Do you work in an environment where lying is common? Can you recognize when you are being lied to? Why do people lie? As a police officer, I work in an environment where I expect to be lied to. One of the most critical skills for law enforcement officers to learn is recognizing and detecting a lie. During an interview with a suspect, an investigator must sometimes draw out the truth by confronting a lie. Other times, it's best to document the lies being told, and then use those lies against the suspect in a court of law.

What I have learned during my career is that generally, people do not like being questioned. Even if they are lying, they do not want their lies to be exposed. When a suspect realizes they are in over their head, they attack the one questioning them. They get defensive and attempt to redirect the conversation to the officer's audacity to confront them. A good investigator can get through this resistance, primarily because the suspect is not free to leave during the questioning. And a suspect's resistance is usually his or her last stand before a confession.

In regular human interaction (other than police encounters), people lie. Anyone who has been a parent knows this. Anyone who has engaged in politics knows this. Anyone who has worked in corporate America knows this. Anyone who has gone to church knows this. Wait, Do Christians lie? While my last statement and question may be controversial, I believe (and most reading this probably believe) that the answer is yes, sometimes they do. Imagine your pastor greeting you on a Sunday morning, asking about your week, and you tell him something he knows is not true. Would you appreciate it if your pastor said, "Now, I just spoke to Bob, and he told me a different story. Are you lying to me?" How would that go over, even if he is right?

If we lie, we expect people to accept it, but why is this true? The writer of Hebrews gives us a better understanding of this. Sin lies to us; it deceives us. Sin has a way of telling us something untrue and sucking us into believing it. Sin always seizes its opportunity to deceive (Romans 7:11). Sin tells us it is all right to lie, just this one time. Then, when we give in, sin changes its tune and calls us a hypocrite. Sin only lies—it never exposes the truth. So, when someone calls us out for lying, sin works against us to keep our lie concealed, allowing it to simmer deep inside our soul. Sin wants to remain in the dark.

Over time, sin's deceitfulness hardens you. That's its goal. Sin wants you to withdraw. At first, you are sensitive about what you are hiding. You feel remorse and embarrassment for what you have done. Your sin may be theft from your place of employment or a flirtatious extramarital relationship with a friend, neighbor, or co-worker. But your second sin is the lie you use to cover it up. You try to deal with it, discussing it with God, but it starts eating away at you. You begin to withdraw because you do not want your sin or lie to come to the surface. You know God forgives you, but sin keeps telling you more lies.

Pressured by guilt, you pray again for forgiveness. Then sin replies with a hefty blow, "Do you not even have enough faith to believe that you were forgiven the first time you prayed?" If you believe this lie, your guilt gets worse. You repent with a pure heart. But that is when sin's deceitfulness takes it to a new level. When faced with another opportunity, sin may say, "Hey, you know God will forgive you, just like he did last time." Sin will lie to you with this bit of truth to get you to come back to it. Beware of this; sin wants you to return. The serpent said to Eve, "You surely will not die" (Genesis 3:4). Sin knows how to twist the truth, and it always deceives. It never tells the whole truth.

If you return to sin, it will work doubly hard on you. The guilt will be worse, and the lies will be fierce. It desires you. God said to Cain, "Sin is crouching at the door. Its desire is for you, but you must rule over it" (Genesis 4:7). The Hebrew word used for desire refers to a craving, as if stretching out for something. Does that not describe sin perfectly? Sin is stretching out its hand persistently. The more we succumb to its desire, the shorter its hand needs to be. Sin's strategy is to deceive us to harden us, so that we lie to ourselves and continue to sin.

Most people who leave the church don't do so because the music is too loud or the request for money is too often. Most people leave because they are living in the shadows of sin's deceitfulness. They withdraw in fear of being exposed. This is what sin wants. What is the remedy for this problem? Truth Exposed. Truth is liberating but requires exposure to set us free. It is difficult to get through walls put in the way by those who do not want their sin to be known.

The purpose of exposure is not to embarrass. That's sin's job. Sin lies to you and tells you that exposure would be a bad move on your part. Sin tells you the rest of us are no better or worse. Sin tells you that judgment will follow if you expose this. It may, but shame on us if it does. If exposure of sin leads us to the judgment of you, then sin also has a grip on us. The purpose of exposure is freedom. The writer says, "Exhort one another every day." Accountability and corporate responsibility must be restored among the body of believers. But this does not suggest we walk around like pious priests pointing out everything we think is wrong with someone.

I believe this instruction commands us to engage with people in honest relationships, sharing an interest in one another and reminding them of their identity in Christ. We must counter the deceitfulness of sin with truth. However, we must speak of liberation from sin as the reason for the exposure of sin. Even in law enforcement, as an interviewer, I have witnessed people being set free through confession of their misdeeds. I have seen many come forth, willing to pay the consequences for their actions because they want emancipation from the hardness of their hearts.

What if we, followers of Jesus Christ, could live in freedom, without guilt or shame? What if sin's extended arm was out of reach because it lost its appeal to us? What if we knew what it offered and had no interest in letting it stake a claim in our lives? What if we never need to live on the run and come to Christ in honest confession, and experience peace? If that were to happen, we, the church, must be ready for it with open arms, grace, and forgiveness. We must not allow sin to deceive us, too. Let's pray for this kind of revival.

Getting Called Out

"Formerly he was useless to you, but now he is indeed useful to you and to me" (Philemon 1:11).

A surreal scenario

Imagine for a moment that you have a dispute with someone, a personal matter causing you heartache. You conclude that it is nobody's business how you feel about that person or what you decide to do about it. When you get to church on Sunday, you notice everyone who arrived before you is looking at you, but you do not know why. You receive a church bulletin, and when you sit down to read it, you discover your name is headlined, and it is addressing you personally on this private, unsettled matter in your life.

Feeling embarrassed, ashamed, and angry, you begin to piece together what happened. Apparently, during the week, your pastor met with the person with whom you are disputing. That person decided to ask the pastor for help in resolving the conflict, and the pastor felt the issue should come to the surface and be exposed. In essence, the leader of your church has called you out—wow.

It happened

This is what happened to Philemon, an influential member of the Colossian church. He had a slave named Onesimus, which ironically means "useful." Onesimus abandoned Philemon and eventually came upon the apostle Paul. Paul helped him discover the life-giving gospel of Jesus Christ, and Onesimus became transformed by His grace. Their meeting occurred at a time when Paul was under arrest. Onesimus became useful to Paul, but Paul knew there was unfinished business to be done. Onesimus would need to go back to Philemon. I am sure Onesimus told Paul that Philemon would not be happy with him. But Paul knew that Philemon had also come to know of the grace given through the message of the gospel.

Paul wrote a letter addressed to Philemon that we can read today. It is a short letter but packs a pretty good punch. Paul's appeal to Philemon begins with a truth—that we belong to each other in the faith. Paul's point in the letter was that God's grace had radically transformed Onesimus, and Paul was sending him back to his master. For the sake of the entire church, Paul appeals to Philemon to forgive Onesimus and take him back as a brother rather than as a slave. Apparently, Onesimus was a bondservant, so he would have eventually paid his debt and left Philemon anyway. Paul's plea makes the argument that as a brother, Onesimus would be with Philemon forever. Paul knew that Philemon's forgiveness would display the power of the grace of God in the church.

Paul's lesson

Today, what do people outside of the church say about people in the church? Perhaps some congregations have a reputation for being judgmental or legalistic. Maybe others are known for being full of grace and forgiveness. What is your contribution to either of these reputations? Do you hold resentment or a lack of forgiveness toward another in the church? If so, have you ever considered your effect on the church body as a whole? What if our opening scenario actually played out, and your pastor wrote a letter to the entire congregation highlighting this conflict? Would it cause you to desire forgiveness and reconciliation, or would you become angry with the pastor and leave the church?

Paul took a risk in writing this letter. As a follow-up, Paul boldly told Philemon to get his guest room ready, because he hoped to pay a visit to Colossae and planned to stay at his house! Well, that would be an awkward visit if Philemon couldn't find it in himself to forgive Onesimus. But Paul understood that these personal matters are public matters to the body of Christ. If someone were to say that forgiveness takes time, they would be wrong. Forgiveness takes grace.

I am sure Paul's intention was not to embarrass Philemon. Perhaps Onesimus felt his abandonment of Philemon would result in his death. Maybe Onesimus needed an influential advocate to speak on his behalf, and Paul certainly fit the bill. Ultimately, I believe Paul's intent in writing this letter to reconcile these two men was for the good of the church body. For the sake of our own church body, we must be reconciled to one another. For the sake of those watching us, we must be motivated by grace and display that grace in every relationship.

Slow Growth

"The Lord your God will clear away these nations before you little by little. You may not make an end of them at once, lest the wild beasts grow too numerous for you" (Deuteronomy 7:22)

The Lord is not intimidated by a process, as long as the process does not inhibit progress. Certainly, a process can be detrimental to an organization if it stifles creativity and spontaneity. However, there are times when systematic steps produce long-term benefits, and the Lord is not in a hurry to accomplish His purpose. Slow growth can be healthy and beneficial, as long as the process does not get contaminated by bad habits or bureaucratic red tape. I have seen people, churches, and organizations grow too quickly only to finish with disappointment and discouragement.

Consider the promises God made to Abraham. He promised that he would be the patriarchal father of a great nation, with more people than sand on the shore, and with land that would be protected by the Lord Himself. Yet God did not appear to move on this immediately. Why do you think God waited? Was it to let Abraham's faith grow first? Was it to allow him time to test the Lord? It is easy to see God's timing in hindsight, but when we think God is slow to act, does it not reveal something about ourselves? When God makes a promise, His word means His promise has already happened. Though we cannot see it yet, will we believe Him at His word? And if He acted when we wanted Him to, would faith be required?

Abraham eventually had a son, the first physical evidence that God had kept His promise to him. But one child does not make a nation, and when Abraham's son Isaac was probably a teenager, God commanded Abraham to kill him. Abraham had grown so deep in his faith that he believed even if Isaac died, God would bring him back to life, in keeping with His promise. But if that was not enough, more waiting would come. Isaac had two sons, the younger being Jacob, and he had enough sons to field a football team.

God's promises were personally passed down to Jacob. He knew what God had promised, yet a great famine forced all of Abraham's ancestors out of the Promised Land. It takes great faith not to take God's

95

promises into our own hands. Jacob could have refused to go, claiming the land as his inheritance. But God reassured Jacob He would keep His word (He assures us all the time of His promises). The promised people left the promised land and moved to Egypt with nothing but God's promise. For the next 430 years, the Jewish people lived in Egypt. At first, the Jewish people held on to God's promise and were warmly received by the Egyptians. But as their numbers swelled, this turned to animosity and enslavement. Undoubtedly, the Jewish people would have given up on the hope of the Promised Land, at least those who had no faith. They probably called it the "Broken" Promised Land.

After the Exodus from Egypt, the Jews wandered in the desert wilderness for almost 40 years. It seems they had a chance to take the Promised Land early in their journey, but the apparent absence of faith caused the people to shrink back and miss the blessing of their inheritance. And although Moses received the Law from God to pass down to the people, a generation would come and go before they would have the Promised Land in their sights. Was God waiting to keep His word? No. He had made the Israelites an enormous people and provoked the land's inhabitants to fear them as a people receiving special favor from the Lord. God had been working His promise the whole time. And His promise was about to be realized as the people re-entered the land promised to Abraham, Isaac, and Jacob.

God always begins with a promise: He will love you, bless you, and multiply you (Deut. 7:12). By definition, a promise is a future event that must be received by faith. We live by faith, meaning we live with assurance in what has been promised because we are confident in the One making the promise. In the case of the wilderness Jews, God's promise included some obstacles they had to overcome, perhaps to test or reveal their faith. The people living in the land they were about to receive served their own gods, and some of their practices might have been quite appealing to a wandering heart. But a tested faith is worth the scars it creates.

As they entered the land, they were tested. God commanded the people to clear everyone out of the land, not to leave anyone alive. He warned them that if they did not clear out all the people, then they would not clear out all of the idolatry and pagan worship. But the appeal of false gods proved to be too much for the people. However, God's commands are not mutually exclusive of his promises. What was true then is true now, His promises cannot be accepted, but His commands rejected. If one believes in His promises, then one accepts His commands. To the Jews, God commanded them to take over possession of the land from those currently living there. "You shall consume all the peoples that the Lord your God will give over to you. Your eye shall not pity them, neither shall you serve their gods, for that would be a snare to you" (v. 16). While this may seem harsh, God knew it was necessary.

Well, we know the rest of the story. The Jewish people could not get themselves to clear the land of all the people. Before you conclude that they were too compassionate to kill everyone, consider what they lost by choosing not to obey. False gods and idols became a snare in the lives of the Jews. Throughout their history, they would battle the consequences of their disobedience. If only they would have had the discipline to avoid those idols.

Similarly, in our lives, change is a process. We will face obstacles in making progress. But God always begins with a promise. Accordingly, the process of transformation is for our good and His glory. Otherwise, He would make it instantaneous. Sometimes, we try to force growth that we are not ready for. Is it possible not to be ready to grow in a particular area? Paul prayed multiple times that God would remove a thorn in his flesh. It never happened. So, Paul concluded his ministry would include this thorn for God's glory. And although the Lord knows our obstacles to change, He is not responsible for all of them. Some obstacles are the result of the fallen world we live in. So, we must learn to discern and avoid these obstacles if we hope to experience the blessings of His promises. If we do not, we may still receive God's promise, but we may struggle to enjoy it. Nonetheless, be encouraged; God is not finished with you yet!

Wear your Vest

"Put on the new self, created after the likeness of God in true righteousness and holiness" (Ephesians 4:24)

After an officer-involved shooting, our department issues a statement to all officers outlining the circumstances resulting in the shooting. These statements are titled, "Wear your Vest." They serve as a reminder that situations escalate quickly on the streets, and officers must be prepared at all times for any possible encounter. One of the most critical steps to be taken for preparation is putting on a ballistic vest. I previously spoke about being unprepared, not wearing my vest. Here, I will talk about the vest's importance.

Though patrol officers wear their vests continually, detectives in specialty details like the one I work in do not. Some details require that detectives dress like citizens to blend in. Wearing our vests would be conspicuous, but they remain close by in our vehicles. My ballistic vest is also a tactical vest. It has many pockets to hold additional gear like a police radio, a few sets of handcuffs, a couple of ammunition magazines, a flashlight, a Taser, OC spray, and a few more miscellaneous items. My vest, when loaded with gear, weighs more than twenty-five pounds.

Wearing a ballistic vest takes a lot of getting used to. Vests are custom fitted so that they cover the most amount of critical space yet provide mobility. Patrol officers wear their vests under their uniform, so when I first came on the department, wearing my ballistic vest so closely hugging my torso felt suffocating. But with wear, I soon felt able to take a deep breath. When I took a position on a specialty detail, I needed a tactical vest. Tactical vests are worn over shirts, intended to be taken on and off. The ballistic components are fit into the tactical vest and are no different than what patrol officers wear. When I received my first tactical vest, I needed to practice putting it on and taking it off, since fine motor skills get compromised under high-stress situations. Something as simple as a zipper can become a near-impossible mechanism to operate under pressure.

Because police officers respond instinctively to critical situations, sometimes those in specialty details engage subjects without wearing their vests. Although the vest is for their safety, conditions on the streets are fluid, and taking time to put on a vest can mean losing a suspect. In these moments, officers are not thinking about themselves. I cannot begin to tell of all the times I was not wearing my vest when I responded in a crucial moment. All officers have had many close encounters like this, and we are understanding of one another when one of us is caught off guard. However, in tragic moments, many will question why an officer would confront a dangerous situation without wearing a vest.

The key is in preparation and anticipation. It is necessary to know where the vest is, what condition the vest is in (is it unzipped?), and how to slip into the vest quickly without getting tied in knots and becoming immobilized. Usually, there is a moment leading up to a critical incident when an officer can take time to put on their vest. It may be while waiting for a stoplight to change. It may be while surveilling suspects, waiting for them to pull out of their driveway. With experience, officers recognize and are ready for these moments.

An officer's vest is an essential component for survivability—it sustains them to stay in the fight. There are many days when the vest is worn but is not needed. However, the vest is essential so the officer can sustain an otherwise life-threatening encounter and remain in the fight.

Similarly, in our Christian walk, there are many days when life is easy. We are not encountering threats either to our happiness or to our faith journey. But there will be times when we must endure difficulties and challenges in life. When those times come, we will be glad that we were wearing our vest to protect the vital organs of our spiritual life.

Spiritually speaking, our vest not only sustains us through difficulty but also ensures we will get back up and continue in the fight. Though it may be uncomfortable to refer to life as a fight, the truth is, sometimes, that's what life is. So, while life is not a constant fight, we must be fully equipped for when it is. Too often, people are caught off guard for some of the most difficult challenges in life. They have failed to prepare for them. Perhaps only symbolically, putting on our vest each day is mental preparation for whatever may come our way. While uncomfortable and sometimes inconvenient, the daily act of putting on our vest is a reminder to live prepared.

In the second part of today's verse, the apostle Paul teaches Christians that we are all fitted with a protective vest. Our vests are created in "the likeness of God," made with the best materials, "in true righteousness and holiness." Where is yours? Is it still in the box in which it was sent to you? Is it in your closet? Is it in the back seat of your car? When was the last time you put it on? Do you remember what is in the pockets? Do you ever practice transitioning between tools stored in the vest, so you are smooth in critical situations? Do you practice tactics while wearing it? Have you ever tried running in your vest? When you need it most, will you wish you had practiced putting it on?

In the first part of the verse, Paul teaches us to put on the "new self." To provide a word picture, the new self is like slipping into a custom-fitted vest. We must wear this vest as often as possible, living prepared for whatever may happen. We cannot think that having it if we need it is good enough. We must wear our new self, get to know how our new self fits, practice in our new self, run in our new self, and anticipate situations that may arise which require wearing our new self. Each of us has been issued a new self—custom-fitted and created by the Great Tailor in Heaven. It has your name written on the tag inside. Trust its capacity. Wear your Vest.

Tough Skin, Tender Heart

"They have become callous and have given themselves up to sensuality, greedy to practice every kind of impurity" (Ephesians 4:19)

Tenacity

No doubt, police officers are over-exposed to extreme circumstances on a regular basis. A busy week for a police officer in a large city constitutes a lifetime's worth of crisis in an average citizen's life. A roll-over accident with someone trapped in the car, an armed man barricaded inside of a house, a bank robbery with the suspect's vehicle fleeing the scene, a victim stabbed in an alley, and a stolen vehicle racing through the city all make for an intense week. Combine these events with the more everyday situations like a person refusing to leave a business, an argument between a father and son, a custody dispute, a Pitbull on the loose, and three hours of traffic control on a hot summer day, and it is amazing that officers have enough strength to come back the next week.

When joining the police department, many envision all of the exciting, action-packed calls they will encounter. There is a thrill in the chase, and one must love the chase to do this job. But what brings the greatest joy is the catch. Police would prefer for criminals to surrender immediately and write out a statement of confession for the crime they committed. Unfortunately, it is rare for it to be so easy. An officer must go as hard as the criminal goes and for as long as the criminal goes—from the chase to the confession.

Callouses

New police officers see and hear some shocking things. I would equate getting used to these experiences like forming callouses. It takes time for callouses to form, toughening the skin where it gets a lot of friction and wear. As either athletes or workers, we must develop callouses for protection; otherwise blistering occurs making the affected area almost impossible to use. Callouses help us to keep going, working, or lifting. They are beneficial to us as long as they remain skin deep.

In life, some incidents can cause our hearts to become calloused. Personal attacks, unexpected tragedies, failures, and fights all carry the potential for hardening our hearts to protect ourselves from similar situations hurting us again. When someone has hurt you, have you ever said, "never again," resolving not to allow this to happen in the future? It seems that at some point all our hearts blister, and we innately feel it needs to be calloused to prevent future pain. As individuals, to be of best service to our family, friends, and others in need, we must guard against this.

Another cause of callouses on the heart is exposure to impurities and greed. Impurities are obvious. Everyone knows right from wrong when it comes to what is impure. However, greed is a bit trickier. Greed is the desire to keep anything for oneself, including one's agenda. Greed is subtle, easily able to go unnoticed. But greed works its way through the skin to the heart forming callouses that take away its guilt or pain. Callouses on the heart make us numb—we lose the capacity to feel and respond.

Guard your heart

Protecting against a calloused heart is even more difficult for police officers due to their on-the-job exposure to deceit, sin, and evil. From their experience, they must form a tough skin to protect their tender hearts. They must guard against anything that would harden them because a hardened heart on a police officer comes off as cocky and indifferent. Far too often, police officers are unable to guard against this threat. The hardened police officer then loses his or her capacity to love and care, qualities essential to keeping a family together.

The Holy Spirit works through us from the heart, but calloused hearts make us unresponsive to His prompting. King Solomon wrote, "Above all else, guard your heart, for everything you do flows from it" (Proverbs 4:23, NIV). If we lose our tender hearts, we no longer have reason to build up a tough skin. But God will give us the grace and opportunity to form a tough exterior; He desires that our heart remains tender.

In God's Kingdom, we are all first responders. We will be exposed to situations that require us to harden a bit, so we can keep going. But repeated exposure to these circumstances enables us to respond more instinctively over time. Without repetition, we will never develop the kind of skin-deep callouses that are helpful in continuing. You see, skin-deep callouses keep the world's pain at the surface, preserving our hearts so that we can empathize with others. And when we give it some thought, other's burdens are typically not the problem leading to a callous on our hearts. As an analogy, the leading contributor to heart failure is what we eat, resulting in cholesterol clogging the cardiac arteries. Therefore, cardiologists advise us to eat a heart-healthy diet. The same principle applies when our lives intersect with others—we must filter what comes in. Toughen up.

Waiting

"Then they said to one another, "We are not doing right. This is a day of good news. If we are silent and wait until the morning light, punishment will overtake us" (2 Kings 7:9)

What does it mean to "wait" on the Lord? I believe there is a misconception about "waiting" that has made its way into the mainstream of Christianity. I have heard it said, "If this is from God, it can wait until tomorrow." Where is the call to action in this? Where is the conviction to respond? Is this what "waiting" on the Lord means? Some say, "we need to take time to pray about this," then, over a short period of time, the need for action dissipates. Perhaps, "waiting" does not mean what we think it means.

I understand that "waiting" on the Lord is an important discipline and sometimes very necessary. For example, if a loved one is gravely ill, we pray and wait. Or, if first responders are performing a rescue, we pray and wait. In cases like these, professionals (doctors, firefighters) must perform their duties while we stand on the sidelines and wait. Therefore, "waiting" is an attribute we must embrace during times of struggle or difficulty. "Waiting" requires faith and reliance on His promises and in His awareness of a situation. "Waiting" is more a call to be at peace knowing He is in our midst, He knows all things, and He is in control, regardless of the circumstances we may face. "Waiting" is the discipline of knowing we cannot resolve a situation on our own and entrust our lives to the One who knows best.

On the other hand, "waiting" is not an excuse to not respond. As a Christian police officer, would you want me to "wait" before I respond to an emergency call? Would you want me to "wait" for the Lord to resolve the situation before I respond? I would be fired if I did that, and you would be furious. The Lord has promised to dwell within those who believe. In so doing, He often communicates to us by prompting our hearts. We would typically call this conviction. Everyone knows what conviction is when they sense it.

But what happens when we are convicted to act, but, instead, "wait?" For example, while driving, you notice a stranded motorist struggling to change a tire. Your heart says the person needs help, but you continue on your way. What happens in your heart? Does your conviction to help really build and feel stronger over time, or does the conviction go away, perhaps after justifying there is nothing you can do to help? I would bet that your mind begins to rationalize your lack of response until the conviction goes away. Maybe you even pray for the driver, that someone else capable will pull over to help. In my opinion, when we apply the principle of "waiting" in this way, we are neglecting His call to respond.

"Waiting" implies peace, generally through struggle. However, in times of prosperity, abundance, or joy, "waiting" does not apply in the same way. What God blesses us with He wants us to share. In the context of the above passage, four lepers were left to die outside the city walls in Samaria during a great famine. To make matters worse, the city was under siege by the Aramean army. The enemy's strategy was to starve the people to death. The four lepers remained outside the city because lepers were outcast to prevent the spread of infection.

The men resolved that they were in a desperate situation. If they entered the city, they were no better off than those dying of starvation. If they remained outside at the city's gate, they would die of exposure and starvation. If they surrendered themselves to the enemy, they would probably be killed, but maybe the Arameans would spare their lives. Surrender sounded like the best option. Their journey would likely be a death march, so "waiting" until twilight gave them some time to reflect.

When they arrived at the enemy camp, they discovered that it was empty. The enemy had been scared off (by an act of God). Overwhelmed, they did what any starving person would do; they ate and drank anything they could find. They entered tents and took gold and silver. During this moment, they were the wealthiest Israelites in the world. They started hiding their loot, probably laughing and crying at the same time. They took a great risk, one nobody else would take, and they were surprisingly rewarded for it.

But all at once, conviction came upon them, the critical juncture of our opening verse: "Then they said to one another, "We are not doing right. This day is a day of good news. If we are silent and wait until the morning light, punishment will overtake us. Now therefore come; let us go and tell the king's household" (v.9). They immediately went back to the city, leaving all the gold and silver behind, so they could help the people trapped there. In this case, "waiting" was not an option. They did not even wait until morning. Had they never gone, their people would not have known about the vacated camp, and they would have perished.

Something terrible happens when we don't immediately respond to conviction—we stop feeling convicted. We justify our actions, saying things like, "they abandoned us" or "we're the ones who risked our lives." Conversely, when we are blessed, I believe He always convicts us to share that blessing. "Waiting" is the wrong thing to do. Today, if you are the recipient of the Good News, are you keeping it to yourself? Are you praying that God will send others to deliver it? Are you enjoying the blessings promised from the Good News?

Waiting to share the Good News with others will inevitably cause you never to share it with anyone. In this way, we abuse what it means to "wait." When we are convicted to act and do not, it is a sin (James 4:17), but it may be so much more: we may also cause others to starve, or struggle, or hurt. Today, if you hear His voice, will you respond? Your response is God's way of blessing others.

The Gift

"For all have sinned and fall short of the glory of God, and all are justified by His grace as a gift, through the redemption that is in Christ Jesus" (Romans 3:23-24)

Suppose I arrive at your house in a shiny new Lexus, knock on your door, and show you the car. I tell you the car is yours, that I paid for it, and have the title in hand to transfer ownership to you. Since you are in need of a car, you are thrilled. But you are also a little skeptical and ask why I would do this? I respond by telling you it cost me everything I had but insist that the gift is for you. And though the gift was a sacrifice, it pleased me to offer you the car.

As you come around to the driver's seat and get in, I tell you one more thing. I lost the keys, so I broke the ignition switch and now use a screwdriver to start the car. I show you how it's done, and the car starts easily. Hmmm... now what are you thinking? Are you skeptical? Do you consider the possibility that the car is stolen? Could I be lying to you? You conceive that you could take the car to a dealership and have them change out the ignition switch and give you a new set of keys for a relatively small cost. But a broken ignition switch might raise red flags, with you becoming a suspect for stealing the car. Would you accept the car as a gift and trust that the giver has not deceived you? Would it make a difference whether you know me when I come to your house?

You accept the car but have your doubts, so you park it in your garage for the time being. You need a car, but you are not sure whether this car is stolen. For the time being, you continue to ride your bike twenty miles to work each day. Every phone call you make and every search you do on the Internet do not provide you with conclusive evidence that the Lexus is not stolen. If not for the screwdriver in the ignition switch, you would have no doubt the car is an honest gift. However, because of the flaw, you are crippled by suspicion.

As the giver, I know the car is free and clear. There was no deception. I recognized a need and responded based on the prompting in my heart. I was pleased to give the gift to you and insisted that you owe me nothing. If you would accept the damage to the ignition and just drive the car, it would meet your needs. But the gift remains in your garage, under a tarp. Though it is the solution to your problem, the gift has given you more grief than pleasure.

Paul writes in Romans chapter 3 that every person is flawed by sin. However, God has a remedy for this problem. Since no one can make themselves righteous, and since all have a universal need for righteousness, God provides to each individual His righteousness through the gift of His only Son. But to accept His gift, we must come to terms with four conditions.

First, people must accept that they are flawed to the point that they are incapable of looking good in the eyes of God on their own merit. Even if they are living an obedient life, they cannot counter the consequences of their flawed, sinful life. Many try to live a good life and hope the scales will tip in their favor when it is time to sort everything out. However, obedience without faith never results in a changed life. Until individuals accept their desperate need for God's righteousness, they will not accept the remedy for their problem. For this illustration, each person is in desperate need of transportation but lacks a way to get where he or she needs to go.

Second, each person must accept that God is trustworthy and that His word is always true. When God makes a promise, the result has already happened because His word is that sure. In our example, if I give you a car, but you think I am a shady character, you will doubt the legitimacy of the gift. However, if you know me, know that I am an honest police officer, and a trustworthy friend, you will accept my gift. When I hear people doubt the goodness of God or describe Him as an angry God, I realize that no matter the gift He offers, they will not accept it because they do not yet trust the Giver.

Third, each person must accept that God's remedy is the only solution to the problem of being flawed by sin and that His solution satisfies all legal obligations to those who receive His gift. Since we cannot become righteous on our own, God provides each of us with righteousness—His gift. God put His Son forward on our behalf. Christ's death met every legal obligation that once separated us from God.

Finally, God's gift must be accepted and received by faith. Faith is the acceptance that what God promises, He assures. If God put Christ forward to be sin for us, then He did it perfectly. We cannot pay Him back. But how many people are burdened by their guilt, as though what they have done is somehow worse than what the rest of us have done? In men's ministry (although I am sure the following is true for women as well) I have met many that are unwilling to accept the gift of eternal life because they feel unworthy to do so. They struggle to let go of their guilt and receive God's gift through faith. If only they could be free. They reject the gift because they cannot accept something so valuable that compensates for their moral failure.

It is impossible to receive the gift of eternal life with a clear conscience without accepting these four things. Accept that you are flawed and in need. Accept that God is trustworthy. Accept that God put Christ forward in your place. Accept this by faith. Drive the car. It is free and clear.

Handling Minor Differences

"Now the apostles and the brothers who were throughout Judea heard that the Gentiles also had received the word of God. So when Peter went to Jerusalem, the circumcision party criticized him, saying, "You went to uncircumcised men and ate with them" (Acts 11:1-2)

At one point in my Christian journey, I oversaw a small group ministry at the church we attended. I have never been a big fan of small group curriculum. I think it sometimes stifles authentic conversation by looking for specific answers to particular questions. However, the group leaders were looking for something to help facilitate better dialogue, so I checked out some resources. I found a good video series that I thought addressed some challenging questions and would provoke great discussion. I mentioned it to one of the leaders to consider, and he asked of the series author, "Isn't he a Calvinist?"

I had not considered that this might be an issue for some and certainly was not concerned about it. However, I am well aware of the toxic divide that occurs in the church between Calvinists and those who are opposed to Calvinism. I do not find it beneficial to discuss here. However, if you are unaware of the distinctions, look it up. I will ask, what are we doing to ourselves? Why are we so open to any and all who come to church but so opposed to a particular doctrine some may have within the church? Do we consider it heresy? Do we see it as destructive? Or perhaps, we just don't agree with it.

I still know the guy who asked me this question very well. He is solid, a humble and consistent servant of the Lord. However, his question put my recommendation of this series on the defensive. Should we reject good content for small groups because the author does not think like us? Is there room for differences within the church as a whole, within one denomination, or within one church family?

We often divide ourselves over petty issues. We too frequently choose to draw the line at preference over truth. Our circle of influence will get very small if we insist on avoiding or eliminating the views of people who do not think like us, speak like us, and worship like us. It seems many of us represent a church that is welcoming to all, regardless of one's background. However, if someone new takes a seat, we require that they conform to our way of thinking. Is this the gospel?

Take a look around the church you attend. Did you choose that church because the congregation thinks like you, and you agree with all they believe? Is it the denomination of the churches you have always followed? Does the pastor preach in a certain way that suits you? If you were to choose a new church to attend, but all that you visit have some distinctions on minor issues that you are not in agreement with, could you still learn, serve, grow, and love? Let's be honest for a moment. It is unlikely that we will always agree with each other on every issue. But we can agree to disagree, and we can mix it up and love one another while doing so. By this, the world will see the power of God.

In Acts 10, we learn of Peter receiving a vision from the Lord proclaiming foods clean that the law had declared unclean. Understandably, Peter had difficulty interpreting the meaning of this vision. While still perplexed, he was summoned to the house of a Gentile named Cornelius, who happened to be a Roman Army Captain. Peter learned that Cornelius had also had a vision to send for him so that he could hear the gospel from him. As Peter spoke to all who were present with Cornelius, his vision started making sense to him. Apparently, the Lord wanted Peter to figure this out on his own, without directly stating that the vision was given to him to show that the Gentiles also have the gift of salvation.

By this point, Peter had been a pillar of the church for nine years. He started as an ordinary fisherman and became a leading voice to the Jewish people, proclaiming the gospel to all who would listen. The story in Acts 10 reveals that Peter had some prejudices against Gentiles. Peter was uncomfortable going to the house of Cornelius. He understood that his contemporaries would not approve of him doing this. In fact, after the conversion of the first Gentiles, Peter did not immediately go back to Jerusalem to tell the other apostles about it. However, word traveled back to them before Peter arrived.

By the time Peter returned to Jerusalem, the established church was waiting and ready to criticize him. They focused on Peter's entrance into the home of an uncircumcised man, a Gentile, and worse yet in their minds, eating a meal with him and his family. As I read this text, I cannot help but notice the absence of joy for the Gentiles' salvation. Peter was trying to figure this out himself. He probably avoided his return to Jerusalem because he was not sure how to explain this to the church elders, who were his peers.

Are you comfortable around people who do not think like you? What about worship? Are you troubled with the way some people choose to express themselves? King David's wife did not approve of him dancing through the city. The Pharisees did not like seeing a woman pour oil on Jesus's feet. And the early church did not appreciate Peter eating with Gentiles. These are small examples of people turning minor differences into major problems. In Acts 11, the church members in Antioch were first called Christians. The reason for this is that they knew no other name to call themselves. Jews and Gentiles came together in the name of Jesus Christ. They worshipped together, ate together, and celebrated their new life together, even though they may have had different cultural practices. May we learn this lesson in the church today.

Breaking Faith

God said to Moses at the end of his journey, "Go up this mountain...and view the land of Canaan, which I am giving to the people of Israel for a possession. And die on the mountain...because you *broke faith* with me in the midst of the people of Israel..." (Deut. 32:49-51)

Moses was a humble man, devoted to the Lord, entrusted by the Lord, and a representative of the Lord. He lived out his calling to the end. Yet, God said to Moses that he "broke faith," and there were consequences for doing so. What does it mean to "break faith"?

I have come to understand this phrase a bit differently when researching how to train a sheepdog. A sheepdog is placed, as a puppy, amid a few sheep, including a newborn lamb. A bond is formed over time as the sheep get used to the presence of the dog. But the puppy's placement with the sheep is not so that it becomes one of the sheep. No, the pup is in training to live out its purpose. It will be a sheepdog working under the oversight of its master.

Therefore, the puppy is not treated as one of the sheep. It is fed away from the sheep to avoid conflict over food. Though the pup may rest with the sheep, it is taught to sleep at a distance from its flock. Through a process of constant instruction, the pup matures.

The shepherd (the dog's master) knows how to train the dog for service. He knows when the dog is ready for advanced training and when it can handle its independence. Freedom is essential for a sheepdog. Without it, the dog cannot live out its potential. However, freedom has risks. If a sheepdog sees chickens at the ranch and runs after the chickens, the dog has broken faith. Once that occurs, corrective action must take place.

The shepherd will discipline the dog. If the dog understands its discipline, it can be returned to its purpose, returned to the sheep. However, if the dog shows a greater interest in chasing chickens than herding sheep, the shepherd must make a critical decision. Likely, the outcome will be that the dog will become a family pet. It will be enjoyed elsewhere, and the shepherd will begin again with a new sheepdog.

You see, the shepherd would be irresponsible if he were to leave a sheepdog among the sheep without discipline, correction, and refocus. It is not cruel of the shepherd to replace the dog, nor is it necessarily a permanent punishment to make it a family pet. If the shepherd can bring the dog back into faith – a faith he has in the sheepdog, he will do so. But if the shepherd fails to break the dog's will, and allows the dog to do as it pleases, then the sheep are not safe, and the other sheepdogs could be led astray.

Now, should there be losses for breaking faith? Yes. For example, a man may break faith by lying, stealing, or leaving his wife. These things lead to a loss of trust. But the question we must ask is, can that man be restored? The answer may be yes, but first, he must submit to the Lord and seek to do His will. Are the losses a punishment? Perhaps. But if the man cannot be restored, he cannot continue to serve the Master (at least not in the same capacity).

Moses broke faith, but he was restored. Were there consequences? Yes, there were. However, Moses also faithfully brought the people where God called him to take them. As fallen men, we all have the capacity to break faith and suffer the consequences. But redemption will lie in how we seek restoration.

Sent out to Serve

"Are they (angels) not all ministering spirits *sent out to serve* for the sake of those who are to inherit salvation?" (Hebrews 1:14)

Learning to observe

When I was new on the police department, I responded to a call for backup for an officer who had made a traffic stop. I had not given the circumstances leading to the request for backup much thought, only that the officer was solo and needed assistance. As I pulled up, I noticed the officer was out of his patrol car, standing near a man who was now out of the stopped vehicle. As I exited my car and approached the officer, he told me he suspected the man was giving him a fictitious name and hiding something.

I should have been clued-in to the fact that this man had a reason for lying, but I stood and waited for instruction as I glanced at him. In hindsight, the man's body language and eyes were conveying that he was going to take off running. One obvious clue was that he started stretching his hamstrings. However, being a new cop, I had not experienced many runners. Besides, who would run when it's two against one? I had a lot to learn.

The officer I came to assist had taken his attention off the man to look inside his vehicle. Seeing I was now the only one watching him and that I was not on high alert, he looked up the street (probably to check traffic), then took off running. After a quarter-mile sprint and climbing over a few block walls, we caught up to the man, tackled him, and arrested him. This foot chase was the result of my inattention, and the seasoned officer I was assisting was not happy with me. I learned a valuable lesson that day: the loudest sounds an officer may hear are the ones made by a subject's body language.

Alert and ready

Thankfully, those days are now long gone. My ability to quickly detect a subject's intentions improved as I matured as an officer and reading body language has become instinctive. Experience provides police officers a keen sense of when someone is about to take off running. So, rather than waiting for the inevitable, I now immediately take custody of suspects and spare everyone the grief of unnecessary sprinting. All cops learn that it is critical to stand alert and ready to act.

It seems to me that angels are spiritual police, always standing alert and ready to act. Angels are on constant watch, staring at God's face waiting for His command to assist believers in need. Much like well-trained dogs waiting for their master's command, they stand ready to serve for our sake and for His glory. And although the holy angels love to do what they are commanded to do, their instruction never comes from us, and they are unable to guard us against evil on their own volition. So while angels serve believers, their eyes are forever locked on God in anticipation of His orders.

The work of angels

Every angel is also watching what is happening in the Church. Paul states, "so that through the church the manifold wisdom of God might now be made known to the rulers and authorities in the heavenly places" (Ephesians 3:10). The rulers and authorities are the angels, holy and unholy. God, through the Church, makes known His glory to all the angels. The good angels rejoice with praise and worship, having a significant role in the Church. The bad angels see God's glory and His power on display through the Church and are incapable of stopping it. The bad angels do not have victories, and they do not have good days. Though they have no desire or capacity to praise God, they must watch the glory of God in the salvation and preservation of the Church (see Jude 1:6).

There is not much discussion on the role of angels in the affairs of man. Some suggest everyone has a guardian angel. While that may be true, I prefer to believe we have the whole heavenly host of angels available if that is what God wants to dispatch to the Church. The holy angels never question God's goodness, even when God commands them to hold back when the Church experiences trials and difficulties. They understand His nature because they are locked on Him, their heavenly eyes in a fixed gaze on the God of the universe. They are not watching us as much as we would like to think. They only see us through tasks God calls them to complete by His command. I would imagine by now the holy angels can read God's body language pretty well.

Our work

I find it very interesting that the God of the Universe chooses to use others to participate in His work. He could do everything on His own and never tire, but He is always including His creation in the work of His creation. It seems that God loves sharing the load, and His angels love to work to please Him. Perhaps we can learn something from the angels by applying their work ethic to our profession. Consider your current occupation. For me, what I love most about being a police officer is that God loves justice and calls on His creation to enforce the law. Whatever you do, I bet the Creator of the Universe sees a purpose in your work. When you work, you share in His work and represent God in what you do. The next time you're on the clock, watch the Creator intently, anticipate what may come next, and eagerly respond on behalf of Him.

Similarly, we can also apply the angels' work standard when we serve others. Certainly, we can see evidence of God sharing the workload of the Church. As Christians, we mature by reading scripture and by learning to pray when alone and with others. Although difficult to explain, we develop our ability to lock our eyes on God in a supernatural sense. So, when we have learned to observe and are alert and ready, He uses us to help others. You see, God does His work through us—He sends us out to serve. What a way to lead.

Peace

"Since we have been justified by faith, we have peace with God through our Lord Jesus Christ" (Romans 5:1)

Have you ever experienced a major earthquake, a massive hurricane, or a strong tornado? These types of events are disruptive and unsettling. People who have encountered events like these have a deep understanding of the brevity of life. They learn how quickly circumstances can change a person's life and the lives of affected neighbors, friends, and relatives.

During media interviews, citizens often share how they felt during the event. Those who could and had their wits about them during the incident sought shelter. They chose a known and trusted location they were sure would keep them safe, protecting them from the potential threat to their lives—a place of peace amid the chaos.

Consider two people during an incident like this: One knows where to find shelter and goes there immediately. The other does not know where to go and panics, often leading others astray. Think about the latter scenario in a horror or action film. A group tries to outrun a threat while looking back to see if they are gaining a safe distance. Inevitably, someone trips and hurts themselves. Then, another goes back to help the injured person. Together, they flee at about a third of their previous speed. If they are the heroes, they find shelter just in time while the villain gets swept away.

In real life, those who do not know where to find shelter need help from those who do. The prepared person may give up their peace and safety to provide it for another. We refer to these people as heroes. We can all agree that the world would be a better place if there were more heroes. Those who are desperate and in trouble are forever grateful to those who bring shelter and peace during the chaos.

As a young man, I had no peace. Internally, my life was like a continuous hurricane. I could not find shelter and ran from place to place to seek it. However, the places I went offered me nothing but more chaos and confusion. A friend recognized this conflict in me and worked for over a year to bring me to a shelter where I found peace. That was in 1988 when I accepted (and finally understood) that peace is found in the person of Jesus Christ. Peace was something I had never known before, but, having found it, I stopped looking for it. Peace came with my conviction, and then understanding, that He is who He says He is. I realized that He did what He promised to do and that He does what He says He will do. I found shelter, and I am still at peace today, grateful to the hero who showed me where to go.

I wonder if a loving God exposes us to chaos, like a storm or crisis so that we come to Him for shelter and peace. I wonder if God has instilled a natural tendency in each of us to seek shelter. Perhaps, trials are how He demonstrates His divine attributes, His mercy on display for us. Consider this: If God made life easy, would any of us seek Him for shelter and peace?

After God brought the Israelites out of Egypt, He led them through the wilderness for forty years. Through Moses, God gave the people clear instructions on how to live as a nation as they came into the Promised Land. Moses brought the people together and announced a covenant between them and their God. The covenant was conditional, giving the people their choice to follow it. If they obeyed the commands of God, He promised to bless them and their land.

But there was another side to this conditional covenant. If the people turned away from God by worshipping other gods or disregarding the law, then they would experience a whole myriad of curses. God's punishment for disobedience intended to bring the people back to Him so they could live in peace. The terms of the covenant (the blessings and the curses) are delineated clearly in Deuteronomy 28.

God promised the people that apart from him, their lives would be without peace. Separating from Him would lead to "no resting place for the sole of your foot," and "the LORD will give you there a trembling heart and failing eyes" (Deuteronomy 28:65). And God promised the people that without Him, they would be scattered from the Promised Land. Does that sound unloving to you? To me, it sounds like motivation to choose to stay with God, where there is peace. A loving God protects His people from the conditions that cause them to run for shelter. But choosing to live apart from God leads to circumstances that draw people back to Him. A brilliant strategy from the Most Brilliant.

I wonder how many awful or unfortunate incidents people have experienced yet chose to run away from the One who provides peace. I believe God still makes His promise of peace to those who run from Him. Continuing in Deuteronomy, the next verse describes the internal struggle of those who do not come to God for peace. "Your life shall hang in doubt before you. Night and day you shall be in dread and have no assurance of your life" (v. 66). A loving God knows how to bring the lost back to Him if only they would stop running.

Have you stopped running so the mercy of God can catch up to you? How many people around us are still running? How many are looking for excuses to justify their way of life? How many are blaming God instead of finding refuge in Him?

I remember having no peace like it was yesterday. Knowing the feeling of living without peace helps me relate to others who are still running from it. I believe a loving God would expose us to a storm where the only shelter that could save us comes from Him. He calls out heroes to show others the way to shelter so all can know peace.

Peace is a gift from God. Every gift He provides is for our good. Every gift He gives is irrevocable. The question is what do we do with the gifts God so abundantly provides? We all have two choices: We can receive the gifts and keep them to ourselves like we store unwanted gifts on a shelf. The other choice is to share His gifts with others. So, if God gives us the gift of mercy, then mercy is to be shared with others. If the gift is teaching, then that gift should be shared. It is easy to be agreeable about these gifts, but what about the gift of peace? Is it given to be stored or to be shared? Remember, He is calling for heroes willing to show the way to shelter and peace.

Who is Your King?

"So Samuel told all the words of the Lord to the people who were asking for a king from him" (1 Samuel 8:10)

God's people living in the promised land were not asking for much. All would agree that the nation was not experiencing the peace and safety they had hoped for. From the time of their inheritance up to this point, they witnessed a steady decline as a nation. Enemies attacked and oppressed them, so the Lord sent leaders called judges to their rescue. But apparently, this was not working very well. Reading through the Book of Judges takes a strong stomach. Samuel was the fifteenth judge. Judges, in those days, acted as the nation's informal leaders. As Samuel became elderly, he appointed his two sons to be judges; however, his sons were corrupt. The people wanted a consistent government that could withstand the test of time. They demanded that Samuel select a king for them, as they observed in other nations.

The Lord told Samuel to give the people what they wanted, not because it was best for the nation, but because they rejected God as king over them. So, Samuel told the people they could have a king but warned them of what to expect. In verses 11-17, Samuel declares everything a king will take from them, stating he will take your sons and make them his soldiers, horsemen, charioteers, and plowmen. Samuel tells them a king will take their daughters to be perfumers, cooks, and bakers. He further asserts that a king will take the finest of their harvest to pay his workers. Finally, Samuel tells the people that a king will take their servants, best young men, and livestock for his use. Then, Samuel ends with a stern warning: you shall be his slaves.

Despite Samuel's clear warning, the people refused to listen, and Samuel appointed Saul to be king over Israel. Although Saul's reign lasted until his death, God ultimately rejected Saul for disobeying His commands. God assured that Saul's descendants would not hold the throne to the nation. So a new line of kings needed to be established.

Eventually, David was appointed as king. He was a good man, a godly man, but he spent most of his life being chased. Even so, he built a small city and fortified it. His son, Solomon, was appointed king after him. Under

Solomon, the nation's borders expanded. He built the Temple of the Lord, and all were amazed by his wisdom. During Solomon's reign, the Kingdom of Israel reached its peak in splendor and size. The entire world looked at Israel, impressed by its glory.

However, Solomon became the king Samuel had warned the people they would get. The temple and all the marvelous structures in Jerusalem were built with slave labor. Solomon imposed a hefty tax on the people. He amassed 1,400 chariots and 12,000 horsemen. The government became strong, but Solomon's heart grew faint. Although he had the opportunity to lead well, Solomon's heart had turned away from the Lord, and the Lord was angry with him. The Lord spoke directly to him twice: he was given wisdom beyond all others in the world, and he was given explicit warnings to guard his heart. But Solomon did not listen. One generation after Solomon, the Kingdom was divided, the people were at war with each other, and the nation never reclaimed the glory it once had. But if Solomon turned away from the Lord, why did God not end the kingly line at Solomon as he did with Saul? The answer is simple: God promised David his line would last forever. This promise never was made to Saul.

Today, David's line is still on the throne through Jesus Christ. He exercises His authority as He wills. He calls people to Himself to carry out the work essential in building up God's Kingdom. However, rather than reigning as an unapproachable king, He leads more like a close friend, giving each of us access to His throne. And regardless of what country or what man-made government we live under, we still have an invitation to live in the Kingdom of Heaven. However, in today's world, it is apparent that many have not accepted this invitation. Some are unaware of it. Others practice a different religion. But many have heard God's Word and either don't abide by it or reject it.

God has ordained the church to advance His Kingdom, but we must remember that bricks and mortar do not build it. His Kingdom is not measured by the accumulation of money, nor by walls and boundary lines. God's Kingdom is advanced when we look to Him and Him alone for all things. He owns everything. His Kingdom is not advanced by those who take. His Kingdom is advanced by those who give because everything we have is His. Is Jesus your King? Are you currently living in God's Kingdom?

Unoffendable

"Many will fall away and betray one another and hate one another" (Matthew 24:10)

When you turn on the television news or open a news app, what do you see? What types of stories are making headlines? Are there many feel-good stories to uplift you? Or do you feel depressed after thirty minutes of local and national news? My guess is probably the latter. I think most people would like to believe society is good rather than evil. So, I find it puzzling that the media apparently thinks that depressing news is preferred over good news. But is society good or evil? We all know there are bad characters out there doing wicked things. However, do we know how bad society is? Or are those who say society is decaying merely exaggerating? As one who tracks criminals up to fifteen hours a day, I will tell you that it is much worse than the media portrays.

However, I do not think that depraved people are the problem in our society. I believe society's tragic decay is rooted inside churches throughout the world—the problem is us. Jesus predicted this would happen. Not sure? Hear me out and judge for yourself.

In Matthew 24, the disciples of Jesus wanted to know when the end was coming. Jesus told them that all of the temple's stones would be thrown down before the end came. This statement threw the disciples a curve as it did not fit their preconceived timeline. They were anticipating an immediate appearance of the Kingdom of God. But based on Jesus' words, as long as the temple stood, the Lord's coming would be delayed.

The disciples wanted some clarification on this. They came to Him privately and asked Him two questions. First, when will the temple be destroyed? Second, what signs should we look for as clues to Your coming? It is worth noting that the disciples understood that the world would come to an end when Jesus established His Kingdom. Matthew 24 records Jesus's response to their questions in reverse order. Jesus begins by telling His disciples what signs they could expect to see.

Now, before I go any further, I should note that some interpret Matthew 24 differently. Those who do will likely disagree with my exposition. However, try to follow me and allow me some grace. I believe that the signs of the end of this age have been on display since Jesus' death and resurrection. Whether these signs have come at an increasing rate over time, I cannot conclude. Regardless, I see these signs today, leading me to conclude that His return is imminent. It is within essential Christian doctrine that we conclude His return could come at any time.

The temple's destruction occurred in AD 70. Many of the first disciples were still alive when that happened. I am sure they expected His return immediately. However, Jesus said there would be signs to look for, and I think it is worth our time to consider what He said. First, Jesus said there would be false Christs who would claim to be the Messiah. We know that has happened. Jesus said many will be swayed by them, drinking the Kool-Aid so to speak. He warned them that the world would be at war but that these wars should not alarm followers of Christ. He predicted famines and earthquakes to occur all over the world. All of these signs are so common now that we hardly pay attention to them.

Jesus told His disciples they could expect hard times, including persecution and martyrdom for proclaiming Christ as King. All but one of the original apostles was martyred, according to historical documents. Since then, many more have been killed for proclaiming their faith in Jesus Christ. Today, Christian persecution and martyrdom are still prevalent. A chart in the 2020 Annual Report by the United States Commission on International Religious Freedom denotes that of the world's religions, Christianity is the most persecuted. And while statistics vary, a report in The Christian Post stated that a Christian was killed every six minutes in 2016. No doubt, there is much hate for Christians in this world.

Next, Jesus said, "many will fall away and betray one another and hate one another" (v.10). I have read this passage for thirty years struggling to understand its meaning. In particular, what does Jesus mean by "many will fall away." Does that mean they will abandon Christ? Will they put aside their Christian journey for a life that cannot satisfy? If so, this poses the question of whether one can lose their salvation. I do not believe God's gift of life by grace, once given, can be revoked. I think this is what grace is all about. Grace gives the undeserved gift of life. Can we return God's gift? No!

I studied the Greek translation of the word Jesus used for "fall away": *skan-dal-id'-zo* (phonetic spelling). You probably noticed the English word, scandal. What does it mean? The primary definition of the word means to put a stumbling block or impediment in the way, upon which another may trip and fall. Its Greek meaning is also a metaphor to offend. So, where do we find a majority of the "fallen" or the "offended"? As a detective, I have interviewed hundreds of people and found there are two types of criminals: those who intend to commit crimes and those who do not. Those who don't intend to commit crimes get caught up in a moment or circumstance that leads to a crime. Road rage, domestic violence, and hit and runs are examples of these types of crimes. Nonintentional crimes occur when people act out of offense. They get caught up, as in a scandal.

Over the last thirty years, I have conversed with hundreds of people in the churches I've attended. I have found that many people have a story about an offense that happened to them in a church. The offense, real or perceived, was committed by a church leader or another member. While some of the offenses were terrible, many were not. I believe these incidents are what Jesus was talking about when He said many will fall away. Trust in one another would erode due to the seeds of offense. Betrayal and hate would take root because of offense. The love of many would grow cold (v.12), and they would leave the church out of offense. In other words, people would act out of offense. They would get caught up, as in a scandal. While not road rage, it's of similar origin. And like a potter shaping clay, every offense taken within our churches seeps out and molds society.

Do we have to take offense when someone puts a stumbling block in our way? Why should we give anyone that power over us? What others do may be horrible. But in reality, we are offended only if we allow another's actions to offend us. We have the choice. Is it possible to do this? When the love of many grows cold, it's seemingly impossible. However, when love for Jesus takes priority, love for others always follows. Love for others manifests itself in an unoffendable lifestyle. But be forewarned: If you choose to live unoffendable, you will be misunderstood, mistreated, disrespected, ignored, rejected, and lied about. You will be hated (v.9). In recent parlance, you may be cancelled. Living unoffendable takes fortitude. But I encourage you to never give the power to offend to another.

If we remain unoffendable, we truly become the city on the hill, the salt of the earth, and the light on the lampstand. The light of Christ will shine through us because the light will point the world to a Savior who is unoffendable. So, as the church, we must take Christ's example to heart. When inside our churches, taking offense to protect ourselves expends too much energy. Taking ourselves too seriously distances us from fellow believers. I have no doubt the unbelieving world has watched us take offense at one another, and they are not impressed. When outside of our churches, we must guard against society's constant outrage at any iniquity, real or perceived. In a society rife with problems and negativity, we must be the group that brings positivity and light. We cannot change God's message in Matthew 24, but we must not be among those who hasten its arrival.

When this World is Crucified

"Far be it from me to boast except in the cross of our Lord Jesus Christ, by which the world has been crucified to me, and I to the world" (Galatians 6:14)

Have you ever noticed how many passages in the Bible keep revealing truth long after you first read them? You might read the same books, chapters, and verses in the Bible for many years and see the same things. One day though, something subtle stands out in a passage, opening the door for a new discovery. Perhaps we should not be surprised at this new finding because all Scripture is God-breathed. But, when these moments occur, it is so refreshing. For me, these instances repeatedly drive me back to the Word, anxiously anticipating another path to follow.

In this passage, the truth revealed is freedom. Paul is writing to the Galatian Christians during a pivotal time in history, especially for Galatia. Emperor Claudius had expelled the Jews from Rome. The primary reason for their expulsion was the disruption that the growth of Christianity caused within the Jewish community. Societal strife increased when a Jew converted to Christianity. These conversions were a huge political problem for Jewish leaders, particularly in their dealings with Rome. As described in the book of Acts, Paul, a convert spreading the Word of Christ, faced most of his resistance from the Jews. In light of the context, I hear Paul rejoicing in the sacrifice of Jesus Christ.

Attempting to keep the peace, Claudius had forced all the Jews out of Rome, including Messianic Jews (those who had accepted Christ as Savior, now known as Christians). Many of these exiles found their way to Galatia. Hoping to keep the disruption from repeating in Galatia, the Jewish leaders attempted to solve the problem by bringing all Christians (including Gentiles) into Judaism. They hoped their remedy would keep the region from drawing the emperor's attention, allowing the Jews to settle permanently in Galatia. Ironically, this solution was stopping the very thing they were trying to preserve, religious freedom. The Jews wanted to be free to worship God, but they were forcing others into their beliefs. They were blind to the fact that they were not free. Ultimately, it was not freedom they were preserving, but compliance.

How often do we see forced obedience happening within Christian communities? In biblical Galatia, the issue was the application of the Law of Moses. Today, it is usually a different form of social order or social conformity. We expect people within our church to behave a certain way. We believe, both individually and collectively, that we have figured out how proper behavior looks. But this focus on compliance creates a mindset that stifles the freedom we have in Christ.

Through Christ, God did what the law could not do. By subjecting His Son to a sacrificial human life, God placed all sin on His broken flesh. Jesus's sacrifice allowed for the fulfillment of the law. But Jewish factions opposed to Christianity were trying to force Christians to adhere to the law. While Christ offered freedom, the Jews were driving Christians into legalistic slavery. Why would they do this? After the Jews were forced to leave Rome, compliance with the law was the key to their way of life. Rome had no issues with adherence to Jewish law. However, once Christ offered them new freedom, a threat was posed to Rome. Paul wrote his letter to the Galatians opposing the Jewish plan. His words were provocative; freedom in Christ meant unwanted attention from Rome.

When you consider Christ on the cross, what comes to your mind? Does it make you feel uncomfortable? Do you feel guilty for being a sinner? Do you ever feel indebted to Christ? Do you feel the weight of guilt lifted from you? Has Christ's death allowed you to live freely?

In your church home, do you feel a sense of freedom? Does your church expect you to comply with everyone else? When you disagree with a stance in the church, do you remain silent to avoid making waves? In a place designed to celebrate our freedom in Christ, do you feel free? There is an irony at play when freedom threatens deeply rooted establishments.

Outside of church, our freedom may be stifled by worldly concerns. Society expects compliance and order. After all, aren't we supposed to "keep up with the Joneses"? Many of us pursue what everyone else pursues. We are taught to stay in our lane so those around us will accept us. If we are not careful, our pursuit becomes our identity. But how are those who rebel against the system viewed? Are they regarded as problematic, defiant, difficult, or disruptive? Do you know someone like this? Do they see liberty and freedom to be what they believe they ought to be? More importantly, do you privately wish to have their independence but are fearful of the consequences?

As I look closer into this passage in Galatians, I see Paul expressing the same sentiment. "Far be it from me to boast *except* in the cross of our Lord Jesus Christ." Paul is saying: I want to boast about the freedom He died for. I want to brag about breaking the chains I am no longer living in. I want to boast about escaping the bondage of expectation and compliance. The next phrase of the verse is as profound as it is provocative. Paul, referring to the cross, says, "by which the world has been crucified to me." This world was dead to Paul, regarding its expectations placed on him.

Christ died to set Paul free. This freedom released Paul from the grip of expectations and demands. The world had been crucified to Paul, and as he adds, "I to the world." Paul, through his freedom in Christ, had no needs and no expectations from the world. Freedom is provocative, especially to those who live in fear of it. Paul did not expect respect or appreciation from those who pushed for compliance and order. Paul stood in the gap for the church in Galatia, fighting to keep them free, a fight worth fighting.

Have you been set free? If you answer yes, deeply consider if you really are free? In your church, do you do what you do because you are free? Do you do what you do because it is morally right and spiritually defined? Or, do you do what is simply expected of you? To the Galatians, the issue was complying with the tenets of Judaism. I am not sure that is our application in the twenty-first century. Certainly, many in the church have a healthy understanding of the law, as believed by the Jews. But the dangerous law we face today is our cultural law of expectations and demands and its requirement for social compliance.

If you choose to break free, don't expect the majority to appreciate what you are doing. It's likely you will be warned and possibly hated. However, those who have chosen freedom will understand. Be encouraged that freedom is worth its price paid on the cross. There are no benefits the world can offer you for complying with its ways. The world will entice you by promising peace and acceptance, but the world's peace is not what Jesus died for. Instead, experience the peace that is only found in freedom—freedom in Christ.

So Help Me God

"By this, we know love, that He laid down His life for us, and we ought to lay down our lives for the brothers" (I John 3:16)

Unfortunately, faith is not a typical attribute found among most police officers. Perhaps it is considered a weakness, a crutch to rely on when one has difficulty navigating through the challenges of the job. Police officers seem to keep it all together, vigilant and guarded—at least on the outside. When an officer loses his life in the line of duty, this verse is the most often quoted passage during the memorial service to honor the sacrifice he or she made during that final, fateful shift.

Are police officers motivated by the love of Christ first demonstrated to them and for them? Is this why they willingly lay down their lives for others? Try this: The next time you see a police officer that is not busy, ask them if Christ's love motivates him or her. Tell the officer your question stems from 1 John 3:16. Since Christ laid down His life for us, is this the example police officers use for doing the same for strangers? Let them know you feel this must be the case, that they must really understand the love of Jesus to be willing to do their job. Although we respect that the officer understands the risks associated with policing, few of us would assume they are motivated by the love they are shown in Christ. But what a miraculous demonstration of reciprocal love when that is the case!

As Christians, we recognize Jesus's death on the cross as the greatest demonstration of love—this is the Good News. But is it appropriate to suggest that we should be leading the way in modeling this kind of reciprocal love? When we read this passage, do we think about how it applies more to police officers or those in the military? Do we miss its application to our brethren in the Christian community? We assume those sworn to serve and defend understand this sacrifice. Do we also believe our Christian brothers and sisters understand?

A police officer does not start his shift with the desire to give up his life that day. In fact, the opposite is the case; the officer prepares for victory. In preparing for victory, without knowledge of what will be faced that day, two critical decisions are made. First, there is a commitment to meet the dragon if it shows its ugly face, running in the dragon's direction while others run away. Second, officers will do whatever it takes to finish their shift and make it home. Survival is not the goal since that standard is not high enough. The goal is victory, and the reward is the peace and happiness of family and being able to rest in their presence.

We recognize and honor the sacrifice police officers make each day, facing society's dragons, even laying down their lives for strangers to do so. Does society honor this about the Christian community? If not, why not?

We know love because Jesus first loved us, demonstrating His love for us by laying down His life for us. He willingly made this sacrifice on our behalf. During His entire lifespan on earth, Jesus knew He would die and accepted this outcome. He knew death would come when the moment was right. But He had a lot of living, teaching, and loving to do before the day came when He would hang on the cross. Though He lived to die, He also died to live. His death brought life to others as He knew it would. Every day of His life was an act of love; His love for His Father in Heaven and for those His Father sent to Him. By His life, we know love. What does it look like when the Christian community demonstrates this kind of reciprocal love to one another? What does it mean to lay down one's life for another?

We assume police officers already resolved to this when they received their badge and swore an oath: "I (state your name), do solemnly swear, that I will support the Constitution of the United States, and the Constitution and laws of the State. I will bear true faith and allegiance to the same, and defend them against enemies, foreign and domestic. I will faithfully and impartially execute the duties of a peace officer, to the best of my ability, so help me God."

Do we have any doubt the police officer took this oath and meant it? I believe police officers make this pledge knowing well what the sacrifice and commitment imply in taking it. The dragon is a symbol of everything evil. I think every officer understands the dragon is waiting, anticipating the challenge to fight. Perhaps we respect the officer's commitment because we trust he or she will recognize the dragon when they see it and will engage.

When someone says to me that they cannot understand how a Christian can be a police officer, I wonder what kind of Christian they want to be. I want to be the man who wakes up every day with a deep sense of purpose. I want to believe I understand the sacrifice I am called to as a follower of Christ. I want to trust that my training has equipped me to run toward the dragon and face the threats it poses—because the dragon waits like a prowler to destroy anything it can. I want to believe I am motivated by Christ's love for me and for others. I want to stay focused and give all I have to His cause. I want to start with an oath and conclude with the words, "So help me God." I also want to be in the presence of those who would do the same.

Rapid Response

"Everyone then who hears these words of mine and does them will be like a wise man who built his house on the rock." Matthew 7:24

How quickly can you respond?

Recently, the guys in my unit received rapid response training for difficult and potentially deadly situations. Our instructors for these exercises were members of our Special Assignments Unit. They are experienced operators who routinely put into practice what we were about to learn. There is an incredible sense of responsibility that comes from being taught by these professionals, men who have learned to apply their skills in life.

First, we practiced firing slowly and accurately at multiple targets from a fixed position. Then we accelerated our response, drawing from our holsters and shooting the targets as quickly as possible. A missed shot loses critical time, so we each had to find our balance between speed and accuracy. From fixed position training, we practiced shooting at multiple targets while on the move. We had to advance from one spot to the next, taking out targets at each location. Because movement affects accuracy, we practiced taking a firm stance before firing. This review of firing technique prepared us for the scenarios we would encounter in the next stage of training.

We were taken to what's known as the 'shoot house' at the police academy. Built of concrete walls, it provides a safe environment for practice while using live ammunition. Here, we received one-on-one training with an instructor, simulating what we may face on the streets as first responders. We took turns approaching the house from the outside, peeking in each window to assess the threats inside. Each window presented a different scenario with silhouettes of people looking toward the window. Some were armed with a gun pointed at the window, while others were holding a cell phone or a knife. We had to identify each target and respond accordingly, clearing each room before advancing to the next window. Once we thought the house was clear externally, we made our entry. From a hallway, we approached an open room. Inside was a manikin holding a victim hostage while pointing a gun at us. We had to quickly assess this threat and take the shot at the assailant without striking the victim. Speed, accuracy, and a firm shooting platform were essential for success. Little did we know just how valuable this adrenaline-soaked training in a controlled environment would be.

Just a couple of days later, our unit identified a man who had been on a spree of armed robberies throughout the city. Two people were shot during his crimes. We were checking out some possible addresses for the suspect when another robbery occurred. Patrol officers saw the man fleeing the scene in a stolen vehicle. The patrol units pursued the car until we, as unmarked units, could arrive and tail him with the help of a police helicopter.

In situations like this, once the unmarked units arrive and are in place, the marked units fade back. A suspect who believes he has escaped pursuing officers will typically slow down and blend into traffic. This maneuver helps to assure the safety of unwitting citizens on the road. It also provides an opportunity for police to get close, displacing civilian vehicles so that the suspect is surrounded without his knowledge. With a covert pursuit in place, special operators with advanced tactical skills prepare to immobilize the suspect's vehicle.

Once our suspect took a road with few citizens nearby, the unmarked officers crashed into the suspect and pinned him in the vehicle on the driver's side. He crawled out of the passenger door, armed with a semi-automatic handgun with an extended magazine protruding from the grip. As he raised the gun toward the officers on the scene, one of the guys on my unit was ready. Standing firm with his weapon pointed at the suspect, he fired once, striking the suspect with precision, and ending the threat. Everything practiced just one week earlier was applied by this officer. Without practice, it is hard to imagine any officer's response would have had the same results.

How quickly can you respond to God's Word?

When you hear, do you respond? Do you accurately identify the targets and respond accordingly? How is your footing? Are you set, stable, and firm in your stance? If God's Word is like our shoot house, where is your practice applicable in real life? We cannot live our lives practicing for something yet never stepping out to apply what we know we need to do! Jesus said, "Why do you call me 'Lord, Lord,' and not do what I tell you? Everyone who comes to me and hears my words and does them, I will show you what he is like: he is like a man building a house, who dug deep and laid the foundation on the rock" (Luke 6:46-48a). If our quiet time with the Lord is like practice for life, where is our life application?

Suppose you need to forgive. Do you identify those whom you need to forgive, and respond accordingly? Do you accomplish what you set out to do? What if you hear that God gives us a purpose, endowing us with a spiritual gift to be dispensed on others for their benefit? How would you respond? Some may say they are not ready for that yet; they do not know enough or that their personal lives are not in order. Others may say they don't know how God gifts them. But in reality, they do little to find out. Some go through life preparing for nothing, building on nothing, anticipating nothing. Jesus knows that those who live like that are like the one who builds a house without a foundation. Storms come, the house falls apart, and the loss is devastating.

Are you prepared for today? If not, I would encourage you to identify areas where you need extra training. Let someone know that you need to get in some reps so that your proficiency develops. Talk to someone who knows how to do what you believe you should do. Find someone doing life well, someone who responds quickly with accuracy and a firm footing. Those people may not be the most polished communicators or even the most enjoyable people to be around. But they live their lives in response to what they hear. We benefit when we see people living as we believe we ought to live.

When we delay our response, we usually end up not responding at all. When we condition ourselves not to react, we are developing habits that assure we never do. This cycle must be broken. We must learn to hear, practice what we should do, and respond. If we condition ourselves in this way, we become like those who build a house on a firm foundation.

Gut Check

"Where jealousy and selfish ambition exist, there will be disorder and every vile practice" (James 3:16)

My wife, Nicole, and I have been married now for over twenty-eight years. We met at Bible college in Canada in 1991 when she was just eighteen years old. She was in her first year, I in my second. I was considerably older than most of the other students because I had attended four years of university before starting Bible college. I was ready to find someone to live out the rest of my life with, and she was ready to start living life as an adult for the first time.

She was beautiful, kind, gentle, and soft-spoken (by the way, she still is). She had a subtle, controlled laugh, always recognizing the subtleness of my dry sense of humor. I fell in love with her and eventually asked her to marry me. Her decision was no small commitment. Marriage would require her to leave her family and native country of Canada, apply for permanent residence on foreign soil, raise children away from her family, and eventually take on U.S. citizenship.

Needless to say, Nicole had to surrender many of her dreams and aspirations to marry me. I believe I failed to understand this for many of our early years in marriage. Being married to me in those first years was probably like trying to read a novel while sitting in a washing machine during the spin cycle. Every day I was pushing Nicole to change. I did not give her time to adjust to these significant changes, nor was I sensitive to her. I relentlessly pressed her to "grow up." The first ten years of our marriage were rough.

Back then, I wondered what was happening to us? Why were we not adjusting into a single unit, working together on the same page? I now believe there were two reasons for this. First, I was selfish and wanted Nicole to make the necessary adjustments so that I could have what I wanted. Second, Nicole was not selfish, and I failed to recognize the stability her unselfishness gave our marriage. I was trying to fix our marriage, but all I was doing was contributing to the disarray associated with selfish ambition. Nicole wasn't resistant to change, but she was resistant to the disorder I was creating while demanding change.

I wish I could say that I saw the light after ten years and that we have been sailing smoothly ever since, but I would be a liar. I did realize how selfish I was, and though I did make some critical and necessary changes, I also caused a lot of damage. Some of that damage crept into the next ten years of our marriage. Nicole would quickly notice some of the same old attitudes from my past and would shut down relationally. I would often react to the wall she would put up, trying to tear down the blocks she was stacking. I think the difference in the second decade of our marriage was my realization of the damage I was doing and would continue to do if I didn't change my selfish ways. I now understand what she was doing by putting up a wall. She was protecting the progress that we had made and that selfish ambition often destroys.

I cannot help but wonder how many years I wasted trying to fix something that was not broken. Nicole does not have an ounce of selfishness in her. It all came from me. I was the one who created the disorder. I created confusion and instability for a young woman from who I asked so much. She had so many major adjustments to make for accepting my hand in marriage. But I just kept throwing more and more at her, prohibiting her from adapting to things like raising our kids in a foreign country and not having her family present to witness their childhood milestones.

Why would I unveil such failure in my marriage? Because I would feel like a hypocrite if I did not. But more than that, based on what I have observed both as a police officer and a pastor, my experiences are really not that unique in relationships. Over time, I began to see a lot of myself in the homes I entered as a police officer to keep the peace. The people I met were honest and often humiliated by my presence. Many of them were middle-class families like most of us. However, they had reached a point in their marriage where one of them felt the need to call for police intervention. Usually, there was no crime committed in these homes. They just needed a referee. These experiences have certainly helped me better understand what I encounter in ministry.

Partly because I understood them from my own life experience, and partly due to my training, I found I could relate to them in their struggle. They had reached a low point and needed perspective. They needed someone to show them that their selfish ambition was the source of their

148

conflict. They needed to put their own desires aside to achieve peace. Sometimes, that was not possible, and inevitably somebody was arrested. I was often frustrated that their problems had reached that level, not because I had to book somebody into jail, but because their damaging choices limited the possibility for reconciliation.

What if we all had someone standing in our living room mediating conflict and pointing out how selfish desire is causing chaos and division in our home? What if we had someone who represents law but not judgment, someone who hopes for peace but cannot force it. James, the brother of Jesus, wrote to the believers scattered throughout the region, warning them of the damage caused by bitterness and selfish ambition. He did not mince words when he wrote, "where jealousy and selfish ambition exist, there will be disorder" (James 3:16).

Marriage is supposed to be a small taste of what Heaven will be like. God designed it to be that way. Marriage can be the image of Heaven when we put aside our ambition and live in peace with one another, in mutual and reciprocal love, being accountable to all who share in it. Marriage can be the perfect image of what Heaven will look like when we live in unity with one another. I am so grateful for Nicole: she always models this image for me, even when I don't.

Expanding on the imagery of marriage, the Church is the Bride of Christ. When we heed James' warning and put aside our selfish ambition and live in unity with one another, there is order, not chaos. The message of the Gospel is then made clear to all who are watching and need a bit of stability in their lives.

One's Perspective on Hope

"Let us hold fast the confession of our hope without wavering, for He who promised is faithful" (Hebrews 10:23)

Consider for a moment a statement you once heard that has been etched into your memory ever since. You may be able to remember where you were and who said it to you. Perhaps, it changed your life or redirected your focus. Maybe you have shared it with others as a great life lesson worth passing on. Or maybe, it was just so funny that it was unforgettable. While it's impossible to recall everything heard in your lifetime, some things seem to remain.

When I joined the police department, just before entering the police academy, the recruitment sergeant called a meeting with the new recruits. He began by asking each of us our reason for choosing a career in law enforcement. As each person around the room stated their purpose, the sergeant listened. When all were finished, the sergeant said something that I will never forget: "If you think you are going to make a difference in this world, you are going to be disappointed. You will not make the difference you think you will. By the end of your career, there will be just as much crime on the streets as there is today. You will not reduce the crime rate one bit."

I was shocked and a bit disappointed to hear this. Like many of the recruits, I had stated that I hoped to make a difference through this noble profession. In fact, I would go so far as to say I was defiant; I believed the sergeant did not know who he was talking to. His statement became a rallying cry for me to push harder and remain focused on changing the world. I had hope that I could make a difference. Early in my career, I was assigned to a unit that focused on apprehending repeat offenders, career criminals. Statistically, career criminals are responsible for roughly eighty-five percent of the crimes committed. I wanted to catch them all.

When I became a detective, my assignment was to identify, locate, investigate, and arrest repeat offenders of serious offenses. Initially, I covered surveillance, then later transitioned into handling cases for prosecution. I worked closely with the county attorneys to apply what's called enhanced prosecution against these criminals, limiting the chance of a plea bargain to a lesser offense and jail term. While on this assignment, I worked for four and a half years and maintained a database on every offender I turned over for enhanced prosecution. During this time, I handled 640 repeat offender cases. The average prison sentence received by each was eight years. Do the math.

I later transitioned back to the streets where I could watch and follow criminals. Recently, our unit was assigned to a suspect thought to be selling weapons to other criminals. When we executed a search warrant for his arrest, another man was leaving his residence. Both men were arrested and were found to be in possession of firearms. Both were convicted felons prohibited from possessing firearms. Both men were known to me as they had received prison sentences from cases I had handled several years prior. I felt a bit old, then reflected on the words of the recruiting sergeant twenty-plus years ago.

The sergeant was correct. The crime rate has not been reduced one bit during my career. The world had not run out of repeat offenders. My hope in making a difference was shattered by reality. But my hope was created by me, not by truth and not by history. I had determined it was possible to make a difference. I had great intentions and had worked very hard to see this through, but I was ignorant. This reality has not slowed my passion for catching career criminals, but it has dashed a false hope I had. Am I disappointed? No. I now understand something that I did not know. How tragic it would be if I faced the twilight of my career looking back at my effort and seeing failure and disappointment.

How often do you have hope for an outcome that never comes to be? How have you responded to the disappointment? Were you wrong to hope for a better result? Of course not. You hoped for something to turn out the way you wanted it to. Perhaps a lot of variables needed to play out just right for this hope to be possible. Did you give up all hope when you realized it would never be?

The writer in Hebrews talks of hope when he writes, "Let us hold fast the confession of our hope without wavering, for He who promised is faithful." Why do some give up hope in faith? Is it because the Great Promise-Maker failed in keeping His promise? That would never be the case. Could it be that some build their hope on expectations rather than promises? If so, it is understandable why some would lose hope.

Consider a man with an addiction. He hates what he does, but he does it every day. He prays that God would take away the desire that feeds his addiction. Over time, he wonders why the addiction is still craving for his attention. He feeds the addiction because he continues to have a desire for it. Finally, he gets defeated, then disappointed that God did not take away this desire. Ultimately, many who face this struggle give up all hope and give up faith in God to deliver.

Why would God not give this man what he asked, so his addiction would not consume him? Perhaps God knows the man better than the man knows himself. Maybe God considers the discipline of self-control to be more beneficial to the man than the elimination of a desire. Perhaps the man needs to face this desire and be tried through fire in order to be purified. I understand how some would be disappointed if they concluded they could not handle the fire and wanted the pathway to be a little easier.

But herein lies the beauty of hope. Hope transcends our efforts and places our trust in His promises, not our performance. Jesus Christ offered Himself as a sacrifice, paying the debt of sin, our sin—all of it past, present, and future. But if He stopped there, He would have good reason to be disappointed in us all the time for failing to live up to His sacrifice. Not only did He offer Himself up as a living sacrifice, but He also promised forgiveness (v. 10:18) and guarantees it. Forgiveness might be difficult to receive, but our hope must remain in this truth and its effect.

The writer in Hebrews reminds his readers to hold fast, without leaning or wavering in their conviction of this hope. Yes, we sin though we hope not to. But if our hope is in the absence of sin rather than the presence of forgiveness, we will be disappointed. We must not waver in our conviction that He forgives us, that He forgave us and that He will forgive us. No matter how we put it, we must be resolute on this truth. Hope in the promise of forgiveness is transformative in our lives.

Those who place their hope in His promises over their own performance tend to remain in Him. As for me, my hope is in the One who remains faithful to His promises, and He always will. I may not deserve to be the recipient of such grace, but I accept it. Perhaps that is why Paul said, "Faith, Hope, and Love abide" (I Corinthians 13:13) and we "do not grieve like others who have no hope" (I Thessalonians 4:13). Hope in Him does not disappoint.

Not So Green Pastures

Then the word of the Lord came to him (Elijah), "Arise, go to Zarephath, which belongs to Sidon, and dwell there. Behold, I have commanded a widow there to feed you" (I Kings 17:8-9)

A shepherd monitors the land on which his sheep feed. When the sheep consume all there is to eat in a particular spot, the shepherd directs them to greener pastures. If not for the shepherd, the sheep would starve, having run out of food. As Christians, we look at this word picture to illustrate how God keeps providing for us—He leads us to greener pastures. We are comforted that our Father comes down from His heavenly dwelling to lead us to better places.

Would the Good Shepherd ever lead us into danger? Would He ever lead us toward parched land? Would God ever lead us into hostile territory? Let me make a bold suggestion: Not only would He, but He does all the time. Why do you live where you live? Why do you work where you work? If I suggested you are where you are by divine appointment, then the environment in which you live and work is by the hand of God.

What about worship: why did you pick the church you attend? Is it because you enjoy the music or the messages? Is it because you like the people and have made a lot of great friends? Is it because you agree with the denominational distinctions? On the other hand, what if you did not care for the music, or the preacher did not inspire you? What if others attending did not genuinely show an interest in you? What if you did not agree with some of the positions espoused? Could you attend? Could you serve? In this latter scenario, do you think you could be there by divine appointment?

Today's passage has a lot to unfold. First of all, Elijah was a man of God, a prophet. He was obedient to the Lord throughout his life. His ministry began under the reign of Ahab, one of the most wicked kings of Israel, the Northern Kingdom. Ahab married Jezebel, the daughter of Ethbaal, King of Tyre. She was not Jewish. Her father was a high priest of the false god, Baal. Central to Baal worship was the sacrifice of innocent children on the altar. Ethbaal expanded his territory and established himself as king of Sidon after mass assassinations to claim control of the region.

Jezebel instituted Baal worship throughout Israel. Jezebel hated the prophets of Israel, having killed four hundred and fifty. Her hatred for the Jewish people has become symbolic of the evil of false religion to this day. In the name of religion, the Israelites were sacrificing their children to Baal. Elijah was on the run, and for good reason; his message to the king was a strong indictment against him. Elijah referred to Ahab as the 'troubler of Israel,' as he had abandoned the commandments of the Lord to follow Baal (I Kings 17&18). Because of that, Jezebel wanted Elijah dead.

So, when God called Elijah to go to Zarephath, He was sending him into hostile territory. Jezebel's father reigned in this area. Baal worship was prevalent. It was a land of foreigners and false gods. Elijah would witness the horrific slaughter of innocent children on the altar of Baal. Furthermore, perhaps Jezebel's father would discover Elijah was in town and kill him for his daughter or turn him over to her. But God called Elijah to this city and told him to live there. God also made a promise to Elijah, that while in this city, he would meet a widow and she would feed him. She would do so because somehow God would make her do it.

Does God still call His faithful? If so, does He call them to places that may not be their first preference, or maybe their last preference? Consider where you live today. Are you there by divine appointment? If so, why would He have you there? Do you work where you work by divine appointment or was that your call? Faith always draws us to the conclusion that when God calls, He provides. How does He do this? I believe that it is because God's holy provisions pave the way for God's divine appointments.

If you are where you are by divine appointment, consider the trials you may face. How would you handle a hostile work environment? How would you approach a problematic neighbor? How would you deal with an unappealing style of worship music? How would you overcome your frustration that nobody seems to care that you are at church? Would you discover the purpose of your divine appointment? How much could you bear? Perhaps, by faith, you can endure all the Lord subjects you to.

God's choices are not always built around you. They may be to use your strengths to the benefit of others. He has selected you, as He did

Elijah, because of your faith. Recognize God's divine appointments and you will soon see the purpose of His choices. Then, when you accept the trials by faith, the path for you becomes clear, possible, and successful.

On Religion

"They feared the Lord but served their own gods" (2 Kings 17:33a)

As you read the above passage, what comes to mind? Do you wonder how it is possible to both fear the Lord and serve other gods? Modern Christianity teaches that the two are mutually exclusive, that it is impossible to do both simultaneously. Those who choose to fear the Lord reject all worldly objects and practices that the Lord despises. As Christians, we expect this from one another. Conversely, we maintain that those caught up in false worship are not fearing the Lord. This principle is ingrained in us; would you agree? However, the writer was not confused by the two, so let's unpack how one could mix the two.

For context, it is important to understand the cultural climate during the time the verse was written. Israel had been divided after the death of Solomon, King David's son. The Northern Kingdom consisted of ten tribes, and the Kingdom of Judah to the south, the remaining two tribes. God had assured the people of Israel that if they obeyed Him, honored Him, and loved Him, they would be kept safe in the Promised Land they had inherited. But the Northern Kingdom was never faithful to the Lord. The ten tribes never had one good king leading them toward obedience and purity, and there was always some form of idol worship. God used the Assyrians (the great empire during this era) to remove the Israelites in the Northern Kingdom from their Promised Land. Their removal fulfilled God's covenant with Moses that disobedience would result in exile.

By God's hand of judgment, the king of Assyria raided the Promised land, captured the Israelites, and relocated them to the Assyrian territory (v.7). As a gesture of continued punishment, the Assyrians repopulated Israel's land with mixed cultures from their surrounding empire, with each introducing new types of idol worship. While idol worship was not new to the land, the newcomers initiated new practices, and idol worship became like a farmer's market of sorts. If people liked what they learned, they adopted the practice. Is that very different than some forms of religion today?

The people coming into the land were very religious, or at least superstitious. They sacrificed to their gods as a form of worship to please them. Some practices were so devout that worship included sacrificing one's child. So, it can't be said that the people were indifferent about religion—they were fanatical. They believed the gods were only satisfied through personal sacrifice. As the people repopulated the land and introduced new worship practices to a variety of gods, the Lord introduced the people to lions (v.25). The king of Assyria was told that lions were killing his people because they were not fulfilling the requirements of the law of the god of the land. In their view, The God of Israel was just another god to please, so being religious, they wanted to know what pleased the god of the land they inhabited.

To resolve this problem, the king sent priests back to Israel to teach the land's laws as the God of Israel required. But these priests were not pure in their devotion to the Lord. Otherwise, the Israelis may have repented and avoided exile. They accepted the worship of idols while simultaneously teaching the requirements of sacrifices to the God of Israel. And it seems their message was weak because the people's worship of God was no different from their worship of other gods. These newcomers attempted to appease God not because of love but because of fear. The God of Israel was known as powerful; He exiled those previously living in the land and sent lions among the new residents. The newcomers deduced that to live in peace, that they must satisfy the god of the land.

Eventually, the people who repopulated the land of Israel became known as Samaritans. They believed in the law of Moses. But their history was different from the people of Israel. Perhaps they viewed the Ten Commandments through a different lens. The Samaritans may have felt that the commandments concerned Israelites. While they obeyed God's law while in Israel, they did not regard it as principles by which to live. In other words, they recognized the 'god of the land' and worshipped him as they understood the demands to do so. Historically, people viewed gods from this geographical perspective, performing necessities to appease the local gods to live in peace. When traveling, observing local worship practices was done with reverent respect.

How are we different today? Do you know some who attend church to relieve themselves of guilt? Where did this idea come from? I am not suggesting we stop going to church. That is not the problem. The issue is thinking our God requires this sacrifice of us to appease Him. Consider the many troubling issues that have crept into modern Christianity and how many people do what they do to appease God.

God was pleased to send His Son to earth to live among His creation. While alive, He came to know us, dwell amongst us, and eat and drink with us so we could share in knowing Him. However, this was not enough. Jesus spent only three years in ministry. If God intended for us to study Him more, He would have given us more time with Him. John stated that in the short time the Apostles lived with Jesus, it was impossible to record everything they learned (John 21:25). So, there must be something more.

Jesus came to earth to fulfill God's purpose, to satisfy the necessities of God's demands, to appease Him. The death of Christ, God's one and only Son, was enough to satisfy every requirement. His sacrifice was made in our place. When we try to appease God through our actions, we are trying to replace what Christ did with what we think we should do. How is that different from what the people moving into the land of Israel were doing?

Religion is designed by man as an attempt to satisfy God. Religion often mixes knowledge and ritual in a way that God did not intend. Every Easter, I am baffled by the practice I see in some countries where they self-mutilate to share in His suffering. Do they think this appeases God? Jesus Christ taught us about relationships and love. We must accept His sacrifice on our behalf. We should not try to match it with our own form of religion.

Consider why you do what you do. Consider the ways you might mix devotion to God with some presumed ritual to appease Him to satisfy your guilty conscience. How is that any different than what we read about? Learn about the gift of eternal life. Consider how it is found and who provides it. Challenge those who suggest it must be earned. Be careful not to mix fear of the Lord with some form of service. Through Christ, God is satisfied, and you are fully pleasing to Him. Let Christ stand in the gap on your behalf.

Time to Grow Up

"Solid food is for the mature, for those who have their powers of discernment trained by constant practice to distinguish good from evil" (Hebrews 5:14).

Do you remember when you knew everything? You were about sixteen years old. You just got your driver's license after taking the five-minute driving test around the block, passing because you stopped at the stop signs, drove the speed limit, and signaled at the turns. Congratulations. Almost daily, if you did not already have a car, you asked for permission to drive your parent's car somewhere. Your parents would remind you of a few safety tips, and what did you say? "I know, I'm a good driver."

Your insurance company was not so convinced. Rates for young drivers are out of this world. When you were a young driver, can you look back and imagine yourself negotiating with an insurance company, trying to make the argument that you were a good driver and that you deserved a lower rate? They would have laughed at you. Insurance companies have mountains of statistical evidence backing up their reasons for higher rates for young drivers.

When we were young, most of us thought we knew everything and got tired of hearing our parents give us their perspective on life. We thought they were out of touch and did not understand how the world worked. Unfortunately, this attitude often extended beyond the family. We thought the same about teachers and police officers and even our first boss. Fortunately, at some point in life, this changed. As you aged, you began to recognize that you did not know everything and that the wisdom that you heard from others throughout your adolescence suddenly made a lot of sense. You now wonder how you did not see this before. It's a refreshingly humbling and somewhat of a serious moment when you realize that you've grown.

Thankfully, most of us make it through this phase and begin to recognize the wisdom of those who have walked before us. We desire their insight but discover gaining an in-depth perspective requires a long journey through life. We read more and talk more. We ask more questions and learn to discern the difference between good and bad advice. Gray areas between right and wrong fade, and we see distinguishing lines separating the two. We can even predict the outcome of our actions with some certainty. We learn from mistakes: those made not only by us but also by those who we walk near.

Conversely, have you met people who never seem to mature? Sadly, I see this every day as a police officer. Typically, these people develop some bad habits early on and feed those habits while trying to navigate through life. They make bad choices that are destructive to themselves and those around them. They fail to mature as adults. They do get clever, discovering new ways to get what they want, often without regard for others. Could this be the distinguishing difference between the mature and those who are still child-like?

The author of Hebrews was writing on a topic when he discovered it might be difficult to understand. Seemingly pausing to explain, the writer put aside his point and gave an analogy to illustrate the topic's complexity. He did not say the topic was difficult because it was controversial. He said it was difficult because some of the readers had become "dull of hearing" (5:11). They were not responsive to the gospel any longer, and additional teaching seemed impossible. Imagine, as a Christian attending church, that your pastor refuses to teach the Bible, or doctrine, or spiritual disciplines because the people are not interested in learning anymore. What would happen to the church if the pastor only communicated a message that was easy to understand for those who are infantile in their thinking? Likely, if you are growing in your faith, at some point, you would get frustrated.

Consider education for a moment. Why do educators put children of different ages and grades in separate classrooms? What would happen if fifth graders were being taught first-grade material every year? After a few years, they would certainly lose interest. But we would never do that to our children. We test them to find the appropriate level of education for each of them, and we also force them to advance in their learning. Most would agree that stagnation is not the right approach in education. However, when I was in third grade, schools in California tried to institute a new method of learning that allowed students to go at their own pace. It was an epic failure. Fortunately, my parents saved me and moved to another state.

Now think about the church you attend. Does your church take the approach of traditional education? Or does your church leave it to each individual to learn and develop at their own pace, keeping its teaching simple, for the simple? At first glance, the latter method of teaching would seem to be a waste of time. However, my wife and I were attending a church, and upon meeting with the pastor, he said to me, "If you attend here for more than ten years, I guarantee you are not growing." We left shortly after that. We do not want to be in an environment that does not support growth and spiritual maturity. Do you?

The writer in Hebrews distinguishes between feeding his readers milk or solid food. Milk is good for the reader but fails to develop the skills essential for spiritual growth and maturity. Just as we would not expect a child to know how to drive a car, we cannot expect an immature believer to understand how to chew on some of the more challenging doctrines in the Christian faith. The writer states, "by this time you ought to be teachers" (5:12), an expression of disappointment that his audience can only handle the most basic principles in the Word.

What should we expect from a mature follower of Christ? The writer says the mature "have their powers of discernment trained by constant practice to distinguish good from evil" (5:14). The mature are always in training; some training is in an artificial setting, and some is through real-life occurrences. Some training may occur through the circumstances of others. The underlying lesson here is that life is too short to learn everything on our own. Mature believers can go beyond the elementary doctrine of Christ, acquiring knowledge alongside each other without being divisive or destructive. We can learn together, and we can learn from one another.

However, I see one more important distinction here about mature believers: they teach others. This is a sign of maturity, a sign that we've grown up when we gather together to help one another train by constant practice to distinguish good from evil. Perhaps we are in need of more teachers. As grownups, I suggest we discover ways to help people along the process of Christian maturity, and not just in educating them, but in helping one another practice helping one another.

One Thing Leads to Another

And behold, a lawyer stood up to put him to the test, saying, "Teacher, what shall I do to inherit eternal life?" (Luke 10:25)

A lawyer approached Jesus with a question. His question was fair, but his goal was to test Jesus and possibly trap Him in his own words. After all, that's what lawyers are good at. The lawyer asked Jesus what he could do to inherit eternal life (Luke 10:25-26). Was the lawyer looking for the right answer? Probably not. Yet there is no doubt in my mind that this is an important question, whether asked as a skeptic or a seeker.

According to documented conversations found in other sections of Scripture, the lawyer was not the only person who asked Jesus how one could inherit eternal life. Nicodemus, a Pharisee, asked Jesus (John 3:1-21), and so did a young man who was considered very wealthy (Matthew 19:16-22). I find it very compelling that Jesus handled the answer to this critical question differently each time. More so, I wonder if I know the proper response to this question when asked.

Nicodemus was told the answer was in a second birth, a spiritual birth. Although he was a religious leader, this was a foreign concept to Nicodemus. Jesus told Nicodemus that one must be reborn of water and the Spirit (baptized). Nicodemus still did not understand, and Jesus asked him how a teacher of Israel could not know or comprehend how one must inherit eternal life? Yet understanding such a concept comes only from the new nature received from a second birth. Reading the text in John 3, one can assume Nicodemus concluded his conversation with Jesus that day with more questions than answers. But we can conclude that the lesson from the story is that spiritual rebirth leads to eternal life—one thing leads to another.

The rich young man, when he approached Jesus, seemed to really want to know how he could inherit eternal life. It appears from reading the text in Matthew 19 that he had been doing his best at living righteously. He seemed sincere and genuine. He also seemed to have a clear understanding that good, clean living still left him with an emptiness inside. Jesus tells the young man that he must sell all his possessions and follow Him. This answer was too much for the young man to bear. He walked away discouraged, likely concluding that he would never inherit what he was seeking to have. The message from this story is that keeping Jesus at the forefront of our earthly life is rewarded by inheriting eternal life—one thing leads to another.

The lawyer, however, was not concerned with inheriting eternal life. His goal was to make Jesus look bad, to impeach his credibility. Anyone who has ever been questioned by a lawyer on a witness stand understands that the opposing attorney will stop at nothing, attacking your character, if necessary, to discredit your testimony. The lawyer's goal is to create contradiction and doubt. I have no doubt the religious leaders sent this lawyer out for just this reason, to cast aspersions on what Jesus was teaching and create uncertainty in the minds of His listeners.

I am impressed with Jesus' response to the lawyer, asking the lawyer to answer his own question, "what is written in the Law?" The lawyer responded, "You shall love the Lord your God with all your heart and with all your soul and with all your strength and with all your mind, and your neighbor as yourself" (Luke 10:27). Seems like a pretty safe answer: just refer to the Ten Commandments. However, the lawyer included a statement at the end of this command that was not included in the Ten Commandments. The command to love your neighbor as yourself can be found in Leviticus 19:18, easily overlooked amidst all the other laws and restrictions. Turning the tables, Jesus never answered the lawyer's question. Instead, He put the lawyer on the witness stand. He let the lawyer give the answer and then told him he would inherit eternal life by doing what he already knew.

What's the point here? Perhaps Jesus had a way of exploiting the heart, revealing from within what each person holds on to the most. On another occasion, a man wanted to follow Jesus but wanted to bury a dead family member first. Jesus told the man to let the dead bury themselves. That seems to be a strange response to the man, but it revealed the depth of his heart—what mattered most to him. (Matthew 8:21-22). Perhaps, however, Jesus was showing that eternal life comes when everything else dies.

However, the lawyer was not finished. Jesus had flipped the lawyer onto his back, and he was exposed. Not willing to walk away in defeat, the lawyer needed some self-validation to affirm he had it right, that he knew how to love God and others. I believe Jesus recognized the lawyer was no longer questioning Him, no longer trying to trap Him; the lawyer was now questioning himself. When the lawyer asked, "And who is my neighbor?" he was trying to save himself and looking for justification of his beliefs (Luke 10:29).

Jesus responds to the lawyer with a story about a person who needed help (Luke 10:30-37). In this story of the Good Samaritan, the victim had done nothing wrong. He was beaten and robbed by some thugs, left helpless along the side of the road. Who or what he was had nothing to do with the story, although the man was probably a Jew, having traveled from Jerusalem. Likewise, the robbers are not an important part of the story. The relevant point is that the beaten man could not help himself.

As Jesus tells this story, I cannot help but think of the myriad of commercials we see today of lawyers wanting to "help" people. If you are in a vehicle accident, just give them a call, and they will provide a team of attorneys to represent you in suing the other person. And it will only cost you 30 percent of what you sued for. In their minds, perhaps these lawyers believe they are helping people in need. But genuine help comes with a cost to the helper. In the story, two men, whose positions dictate that they should have helped, pass by the victim. The third to come along, someone of significantly lower social stature, stops and helps. Jesus' point focuses on that critical moment, that risky, inconvenient life or death moment when another needs help. The one who responds is a true neighbor.

Jesus never answered the lawyer's question about how he could inherit eternal life. What Jesus did was exploit the man's attempt to justify himself. Jesus put a hole in the lawyer's theological construct. As I read through Jesus' words to this man, I come away with this simple conclusion: Love is our response to others—neighbors— when it is inconvenient to do so. That kind of love must come from above. That love, given through Jesus, is the answer to the lawyer's question. In other words, neighborly love leads to eternal life—one thing leads to another.

An Unusual Pep Rally

Vengeance is mine, and recompense, for the time when their foot shall slip; for the day of their calamity is at hand, and their doom comes swiftly (Deuteronomy 32:35)

Imagine for a moment a high school pep rally. The whole school is in attendance, students, teachers, the principal. The gym is decked out with banners and ribbons, the cheerleaders are shouting and performing their routines, and the football players are on the gym floor wearing their jerseys. Then comes the time for the football coach to address his team. He states: "You guys are going to fail miserably tonight as you battle your opponent. You will not win. You will embarrass yourselves!" Ouch, that may ruffle some feathers among the parents and school administrators.

Now let's look back about 3,500 years. Moses had led the people through the wilderness for forty years, up to the edge of the Promised Land. The Lord gave the Israelites the land east of the Jordan River during Moses' tenure. Moses was alive to witness the beginning of the fulfillment of God's promise of the land He would give to Israel (Genesis 15:18). The Israelites first took up residence on the east side of the Jordan, with some tribes already receiving their inheritance. Knowing it was time to turn over leadership to Joshua to guide the people into the Promised Land across the Jordan River, Moses assembled the people for his final address to them.

Although it's not written, as we read the text, we might imagine that those in attendance anticipated a motivational speech—a pep rally. After all, this was a momentous occasion when considering how long the Israelites had wandered in the wilderness. However, Moses knew God face to face, and he knew something about the people who would inherit the land; when they got comfortable, they would rebel. He knew they would turn to and serve other gods, despising God and breaking the covenant (Deuteronomy 31:20).

So, the Lord told Moses to write a song and teach it to the people of Israel during his address to them. As did the school gathered for the pep rally, the Israelites surely anticipated an inspiring speech filled with optimism and hope to rally them. But, like the coach, Moses did not do that. Instead, the song he wrote reminded them in their rebellion that it was not they who conquered the land but God who provided it. The song's intention was to repeatedly remind the people to turn their hearts back to the Lord.

Maybe it was discouraging for Moses that he had invested forty years with two generations of Israelites in the wilderness, bringing them to the edge of the Promised Land, only to realize they would turn their backs on their God. On the other hand, perhaps Moses always knew that these people were inclined to rebel. Moses may have understood God's rationale better than we think. Moses was obedient to what God called him to do. But his obedience was not measured by results; Moses understood that God had a purpose. Perhaps Moses understood how this chapter in the lives of the Israelites would one day set the stage for the coming of Christ.

The song that Moses wrote is recorded in Deuteronomy 32. It is not encouraging, even though it starts out positively because the story of their journey is inspiring. God plucked them from slavery and promised them an inheritance. He singled out Israel above all other nations of the world. But, at the height of such glory, the people grew fat, and instead of gratitude, they rebelled against the Provider (v. 15). From that point on in the song, Moses focuses on the negative.

Why would Moses be so pessimistic just before the people's inheritance of the Promised Land? Wouldn't such discouragement deter the people from taking the land? Instead, the Israelites got off to a good start. They conquered the land with minimal casualties. They inherited cities that were already built, enjoyed wells that were already dug, and harvested fields that were already planted. That looks a lot like victory.

So, maybe Moses' address was more like a half-time speech: "Guys, you are up by fifty points. I know you think you have this game in the bag. But you don't. Your opponent is coming at you. They will drive you into the ground because you will not be trying hard in the second half. You will give up. You will be defeated and embarrassed!" Even if the other team came back, a coach addressing his team this way would be disheartening.

Now, consider a pastor who tells a young disciple that he will drift from the faith once life gets easy. Is such counsel appropriate? Is it accurate? Perhaps the seemingly easy life is an obstacle to faith. Once one has it, the cost of discipleship loses its appeal. Discipline and obedience are virtues that develop spiritual grit to keep one from pursuing a life of ease. That is not to say that walking by faith is difficult. Walking by faith may become second nature, and it brings peace. However, peace and ease are not the same thing.

Peace transcends circumstances—difficulty. Ease is the absence of difficulty. Life can be difficult, and one can still have peace. So, how does one continue to live by faith, whether in times of difficulty or in times of ease? I believe faith is cultivated through one's perspective. When that perspective is that we have accomplished something, or we credit ourselves with accomplishment, we conclude faith is not necessary. As we continue to succeed, faith diminishes.

All of us need to be reminded that God is the giver of life. He didn't create us to live apart from Him. He designed us to need Him, and we must look to Him for everything. If we fall away, would it be appropriate for God to discipline us to bring us back to Him? Is that love? Moses wrote his song to be memorized by the people. Moses hoped the people would remember the words of this song as a reminder to humble themselves, recall their history, repent, and turn back to God, the giver of life.

Though these words are difficult to read, let them sink in. Understand why God wanted some of Moses' last words to be a warning to the people: "You were unmindful of the Rock that bore you, and you forgot the God who gave you birth. The Lord saw it and spurned them, because of the provocation of his sons and daughters. And he said, 'I will hide my face from them; I will see what their end will be, for they are a perverse generation, children in whom is no faithfulness" (Deuteronomy 32:18-20).

Consider Two Paths

"Enter through the narrow gate. For wide is the gate and broad is the road that leads to destruction, and many enter through it. But small is the gate and narrow the road that leads to life, and only a few find it" (Matthew 7:13-14 NIV)

Consider two paths. One you see looks easy, and the other looks hard. The easy path is wide and smooth, and the hard path is rocky, narrow, and mountainous. The easy path has many people coming and going in both directions, laughing and telling you how much you will enjoy it if you take it. The hard path has nobody coming back in the opposite direction that you can ask about it. The easy path is familiar to passersby because everyone comes and goes as they please, at their convenience. One has no idea why nobody is coming back from the hard path. When you consider these two paths, you must choose which one you will take.

Suppose you take the easy path. You have fun, and you enjoy the company of others. But when you ask people where it is heading, nobody really knows because nobody has reached the end. Many speculate about it, yet each has his or her own theory. The easy path's end is too far or not convenient, and people feel they do not have enough time to take the journey. The path is pleasant, but it is rather pointless.

But what if you take the hard path. At first, you are scared because you are all alone. You see and hear things that are unfamiliar to you. You have difficulty seeing where you are going because the path is so dense. Once you take this path, going back is impossible because of the thick brush. You have no option but to keep going and believe you chose the right path. Continuing seems like an impossible challenge. But, for some reason, you have faith in the path's destination, and your perseverance brings you to a place where you can eventually see some light. That little bit of light is the most precious thing you have seen while traveling along the hard path. You are far from your destination, but hope keeps you going. You know you can make it through because at least there is some light. Turning back would mean more darkness.

On the hard path, you never get to see what the end looks like until you reach it. That's because of all the false summits you encounter. You

175

scale a peak but discover there is yet one even higher you must climb and a challenging valley to cross between them. It takes great determination and faith to face another summit while believing the end is closer. After you have journeyed for quite some time, you begin to hear voices up ahead. They are not laughing like those on the easy path. They are embracing one another with great joy and sharing experiences of their journey. They have reached their destination.

In essence, traveling the hard path requires grit. Those on it never see anyone coming the other way because having chosen it requires determination to make it to the end. The hard path is a one-way road. Those who choose the hard path have put aside ease for the time being. If ease is the reward for this life, they forfeit it for the greater reward that is to come for taking the hard path.

On the other hand, those who choose the easy path think being on it is their prize. That's why they never get anywhere. It is a wide two-way freeway that leads them back to where they started. Therefore, whoever takes the easy path never gets anywhere.

Have you ever noticed that the closest you are to God is during the hardest times in your life? Your deepest struggles are a gift from God, showing you that He can get you through difficulty and bring you near to Him.

Jesus finished the Sermon on the Mount with a clear illustration of the differences between the two paths one must consider. Looking at our verse from Matthew, one path leads to destruction, and the other leads to life. Those on the easy path, try to save themselves by being good. But those choosing the hard path, stop trying to save themselves by simply being good enough. By faith, they trust that the hard path leads to life. Jesus is drawing the line as clearly as He possibly can. If the analogy of the two paths is not clear enough, Jesus gives other examples. He compares two trees: one with good fruit and the other with bad fruit. He also compares two foundations: one built on solid rock that sustains a person through difficult times, and the other built on sand and is swept away when life's storms come.

How can we know the hard path leads to life if we cannot see where it ends up, and nobody who has reached its end can tell us about it? Jesus does not ask much from us. Yet the one thing He asks is challenging.

Against our nature, we each must accept that only He can save us from destruction. So, if we believe this, we must stop trying to save ourselves. What do I mean? If I were to ask you if you are going to heaven, how would you answer? Do you "hope so?" If that is where you stand, you do not have faith that Christ Jesus can and will save you. It is a dilemma faced by many, as it is counterintuitive that one can do nothing to earn it, contrary to conventional thinking. It is natural to think that "certainly, God expects something of me." Yes, He does. He expects that you place your entire being in His hands.

Some years ago, I responded to a call of a man threatening family members with a rifle. When I arrived at the residence, a woman ran out of the house screaming as she was running to me. She ran to the one whom she believed could save her, yelling, "Please, save me." She later told me she had given up all hope, thinking she was going to be killed. When she saw me arrive, she risked her life by sprinting to the door, not knowing if the man would shoot her in the back. She told me she thought that every step toward me would be her last; until she got to me. Then she felt she would live, and she did. For my effort, the man shot at me, missing the top of my head by inches. Though my efforts cannot compare to what Christ has done for us all, I see an analogy here. This woman chose the hard path by running and not looking back and lived. I came for her, and I stood between her and the one who could kill her. I took the shot for her, and he missed.

Consider the two paths. Take the only one that will save you.

Defiant

"If I were still trying to please man, I would not be a servant of Christ" (Galatians 1:10).

If Paul were a missionary today, traveling from church to church to check on its welfare, paying close attention to its doctrine, and examining its governance, would he be a welcomed presence in most modern churches? Paul was passionate about doctrine, always monitoring the waves of cultural influence that work their way into churches, always preserving the purity of the message of the Gospel, and always defending the freedom Christians have in Christ. He called out anyone that he felt created a stumbling block for the advancement of the Gospel. Based on what I can discern from his personality and approach, I think many today would consider his passion and presence to be disruptive. Many in church leadership may even find him defiant.

Throughout the letters to the churches, Paul showed concern for practices that were burdensome to the believers. He called out those who abused the freedom we have in Christ. He corrected well-intentioned leaders who were discouraged. He singled out deserters of the faith and rebuked indifference to sin. He defended his approach by continually reminding readers of the authority given to him by Christ, the ministry he was called to, and the One whom he desired to please the most. Any casual reader of his letters would note examples of his defense for what he was doing and who he was. Paul was comfortable in his own skin and knew exactly what he was doing when he challenged some of the church's orthodoxies.

How do we reconcile this approach in our modern church culture? Are we not measured by how well we get along with everyone and if we attend church consistently? Do we not feel somewhat judged by whether we give appropriately? Are we not often measured by whether we serve enthusiastically? Are we not expected to show reverence to our church leaders on all matters, deferring to their authority on just about everything?

Now, what happens when someone disagrees? Do you think we have advanced in church leadership to the point where we can have discussions with our leaders on matters we believe can better serve our community?

Can we talk about doctrines and philosophies we find to be troubling? From my perspective, many people remain quiet for fear of being labeled insubordinate, defiant, or having a problem with authority. But this fear did not stop Paul when he went before the church leadership in Jerusalem to defend his ministry to the Gentiles. The leaders listened to his concerns with humility. Through thoughtful discussion and compromise, the leaders agreed to make changes for the advancement of the Gospel (Acts 15:1-35, Galatians 2:1-10).

Paul had a vision for the church that would outlive his ministry. He was commissioned to go to the Gentiles, yet he still had a desire to see his people, the Jewish people, come to faith in Christ. I believe Paul understood the conflict in Jesus' day. In fact, since Paul states he was once a Pharisee, it's likely he previously spoke in opposition to Jesus. Do you remember the indictment Jesus delivered to the Pharisees? "You outwardly appear righteous to others, but within you are full of hypocrisy and lawlessness" (Matthew 23:28). To the Pharisees, their appearance meant everything, and they demanded respect from those who could not live up to their standards.

Fifteen years after the death of Christ, Paul was transformed entirely from the self-righteous to the Christ-centered. Then the Jewish religious leaders placed their attention on him, as it once was on Jesus. A target was on Paul's back for daring to speak against the system where the Pharisees were the only winners. Their self-righteousness infected the early church, and some leaders demanded that others live up to the same high standard they lived by. Paul was once one of them. He wrote to the Galatians, "You have heard of my former life in Judaism, how I persecuted the church of God violently and tried to destroy it" (Galatians 1:13). Paul knew exactly how much damage the Jewish religious leaders were trying to inflict on the church. After his conversion, Paul struggled against their passion and fervor to defend and protect Christ's church.

Now, just because you are called does not mean everyone will welcome you. So, what would you do if you saw the church losing its way? Would you speak up? Would you dare teach against practices that you believed were suffocating believers? Would you be willing to offer a solution that promotes unity, builds up the church, and supports the church's mission? By no means would I ever suggest fighting within the church or fighting the leadership of the church. Nothing good can come from that. However, what we need is the courage to do what is right, even when those around us are not.

Remember the story of Shadrach, Meshach, and Abednego. They refused to worship the golden image of the Babylonian king while in captivity. Good for them. But did you know that there were about 10,000 Jews in captivity with them? Yet these were the men who dared to do what was right, regardless of the consequences. The rest followed the masses and complied.

Paul fought against religious leaders, knowing that he would not be popular. But his identity was no longer in what others thought of him. His identity came from Jesus, who called him to this unpopular approach so that the Gentiles would experience the freedom that he had in Christ. I believe Paul would suggest that the servant of Christ is the one who honors Him in word and action, even when faced with ridicule—do you?

The modern Christian church is at a crossroads. Traditional services are not popular, and contemporary services are striving for relevance within this culture. In many churches, the Word of God is no longer a priority when they gather. For the next generation to have a love for God's Word, this generation must show them how by stepping forward in Christ as did Paul when the infant Christian church was at a crossroads.

Conformity

"For before certain men came from James, he (Peter) was eating with the Gentiles; but when they came, he drew back and separated himself, fearing the circumcision party" (Galatians 2:12)

Why do people have a natural propensity to conform to what others want or think? Social conformity is a fascinating study, and many noteworthy experiments have been conducted to show how easily people can be swayed to do what others are doing, right or wrong. I recently watched a study where five panelists were shown a series of pictures, each having varied-sized images. The panelists were asked which of the images was the largest in each picture. Sitting together at a table looking forward, each person stated out loud what they thought, and could be heard by the others. The twist in the experiment was that four of the five panelists were actors, so only one of the five was being studied.

The one being studied sat at the end of the table to be sure to hear the others' answers before making a choice. The actors were told what answer to give as they were shown each picture. At first, they gave the correct answer each time. However, when the actors all gave the wrong answer (even when the correct answer was obvious), many of the experiment's subjects went along with others and chose the same answer. How can that be? Why do the actions and attitudes of others have so much influence on what we think or do?

Putting the experiment into context with the above passage, consider some similarities. Peter was one of the pillars of the Church, especially to the churches in Judea. In other words, Peter's influence, calling, commissioning, and apostleship was with the Jewish believers. Paul makes it clear in his letter to the Galatians that Peter had been entrusted with the Gospel to the circumcised (The Jewish people). On the other hand, Paul began his ministry in the northern cities, not in Judea. Though a great number of Jewish people came to faith in Christ through Paul's ministry, he recognized the distinction between a Christian Jew and a Christian Gentile. Through Paul, a vibrant church had grown in the north, and Peter wanted to check it out for himself.

Paul understood that he, like Peter, was an apostle. However, Paul was commissioned to the Gentiles. Throughout his ministry, Paul practiced what he preached, so he did not contend with Jewish believers as they retained Judaism in their belief and practice. Although he challenged the traditions that were man-made, he valued the foundation and heritage of the people of Israel. Paul was once a leader among those practicing Judaism, advancing in knowledge and discipline beyond his peers—he was zealous. But when he met Jesus, he was commissioned to go to the Gentiles. This would have been quite a learning curve for a man like Paul, being so committed to Judaism.

Peter's ministry was in Judea to the Jewish people. He did not understand the culture of the believing Gentiles. He probably had not given much thought as to how they should organize and what they should practice. Conversely, it was easy to know what to do if you were a Jewish believer. One would just come to believe that Christ was the Messiah. All of the holidays, traditions, and requirements had been ingrained into their lives since childhood. They would need to make some paradigm shifts on issues like their daily sacrifice, but they knew the Scriptures and read through them to see how Christ, the Messiah, was predicted.

People have always looked to leaders for guidance, and as an apostle, Peter had a lot of influence. What he did, how he lived, and what he believed would shape the Church forever. But, noticing Paul's significant influence within Antioch's church, Peter was inclined to travel north for a visit. Antioch had it figured out, mixing together Gentiles and Jews within the body of Christ—the Church. The Jewish believers were instrumental in shaping this culture. They already believed in God and knew how to worship Him. They would need to break free from the suffocating traditions, but it must have felt liberating. The Gentiles came out of pagan culture; they were polytheists, idol worshippers. Many were religious in the worst way. When they became believers, their paradigm shifted significantly. I am sure they enjoyed learning from the pillars of the faith how to worship God.

Peter arrived in Antioch and witnessed the vibrancy of the Christian community. He saw the diversity of those in the faith. This was new to Peter, as essentially, he was the outsider. However, to all who believed in Christ, Peter was a rock star. He was one of Jesus' closest friends; he had first-hand knowledge of everything. He witnessed Jesus' death, burial, and resurrection. He performed many miracles, stood strong in the face of persecution, and witnessed the first converts to Christianity. He was a powerful preacher, teacher, apostle, and leader in the Church. He had influence.

Sitting around, enjoying the company of the community of believers, I believe Peter was the one who was learning. He witnessed that Jews and Gentiles could come together in one faith, one body, one spirit, yet still be diverse in many ways. The believers must have been excited to have Peter in their presence, and Peter must have been thrilled to witness how the Great Commission given by Jesus had come together.

However, some within Peter's closest circle in Judea came to Antioch, perhaps to witness what was happening or to ask Peter to return to Judea. When Peter saw them, he got up from a table where he was eating with the Gentiles, likely before the Judeans saw him. Due to the pressure of social conformity, Peter, a pillar of the church, was afraid to be seen by his peers with Gentiles. Following Peter's example, the rest of the Jewish believers also got up. Can you imagine the shock on the faces of the Gentiles at the table?

There was also another at the table named Barnabas. Barnabas was Paul's ministry partner. He, alongside Paul, had been teaching the Gospel to the Jewish and Gentile Galatians. But by Peter's example, he too got up, conforming to the Judean visitor's social expectations. Barnabas was influenced by Peter and the rest of the Jews, even though they were doing wrong. He was led astray by their hypocrisy (v.14).

Paul knew he had to do something quickly. A delayed response could have had disastrous consequences. He challenged Peter (and the rest of the Jewish believers) in front of everyone (v.14). I am sure he raised his voice a bit. He stood firm that day, knowing he was fighting for the Church's future and for the advancement of the Gospel to the Gentiles.

Have you ever sold out? Have you ever followed the pack just to fit in? Have you ever done wrong because others did when doing right would have been unpopular? Undoubtedly, conformity is part of our everyday lives. We follow fashion trends. We go to parties we really don't want to attend. How about on Sundays—have you ever stood up in church just because everyone else was? Now, we know nothing about Peter's

185

reaction to this confrontation. But based on what I know of Peter from the Gospels, I would guess he took Paul's rebuke just fine. Even though conformity is our natural bend, it is oddly comforting to know that even an apostle can fall victim to societal pressures. Some conformity is natural and probably healthy. But I suggest we discern between the two and be careful not to be swayed by what is wrong just because it is popular.

Why I am Not a Follower

And He [Jesus] said to them, "Follow me, and I will make you [become] fishers of men" (Matthew 4:19, Mark 1:17). These verses are essentially the same except for the bracketed words as read in Mark.

Consider for a moment how the New Testament is organized. There are four Gospels, the book of Acts, twenty-one epistles, and the book of Revelation. The epistles are letters that were written to churches or individuals. Remarkably, and not often recognized, there is not one command "to follow" in any of the epistles. Jesus said to His disciples, "Follow me, and I will make you fishers of men." In Greek, the word meaning 'to follow' is deute. The verb tense Jesus uses implies that one must get behind Him. Duete also means 'to come,' either to a person or event. There are twelve occurrences of this word in the New Testament; eleven are found in the Gospels, and it is used once in the book of Revelation. However, its meaning 'to follow' is only used twice as in Matthew 4:19 and Mark 1:17.

I am struck by this. After further investigation, I found a derivative of the same word with a slightly different meaning. The Greek word, deuro means 'come,' or 'come here.' Jesus used this word when he spoke to the rich young ruler in Matthew 19:21, Mark 10:21, and Luke 18:22. In each Gospel, after Jesus tells the young man to sell all of his possessions and give the money to the poor, he states, "and come, follow me." Yet the command to follow in this way seems absent in the letters. If following Him was important to Jesus, why would the point not be reemphasized over and over again, until all people followed?

Is it possible that Jesus called His disciples to follow until the church was established, and then to lead? This is not a concept I want to get wrong. The mere suggestion that I am not a follower would be considered sacrilegious to most. Christians have been described as followers since the birth of the church, and I believe that is what we are. I believe Christians are to follow Jesus' lead. But for what reason and what purpose? Is it purely for self-denial, to assume nothing of yourself to show yourself to be a Christian?

I actually know a thing or two about being a follower. I make a living doing it and have found a great deal of success at it. By definition, I am in the surveillance business, working in a police unit that follows criminals. I work undercover so that I blend into society to avoid detection. When criminals are out and about, so am I, following them wherever they may go, such as into stores, restaurants, casinos, and gas stations. The officers in my unit change clothes and appearance so that criminals are not able to recognize us. We also use technology to assist us, to help us follow. In any given week, I am following either a criminal or an associate for as many as fifty to sixty hours.

However, we follow with a purpose. There is nothing random about our job. We watch and learn behaviors, predictive behaviors, that serve as clues to when perpetrators are about to offend. Observing these indicators, we begin calling in additional assets, ready to transition from surveillance to apprehension. Without the belief that these people would re-offend, we would not follow them. So essentially, following is not our purpose; it is our discipline so we can accomplish our mission to catch a criminal.

Following is exhausting, and it is the riskiest aspect of my job. Sometimes, in order to follow someone, we may need to get through intersections at a red light, get around a train stopping traffic, or get ahead of a suspect's vehicle, all while avoiding detection. If one of us is caught following, the rest of us are compromised. I have personally watched subjects point weapons at co-workers after being detected. The risks are necessary to be effective as a follower. Still, the mission transcends the task. We follow to catch criminals. Take that aspect out of our job, and the risks would not be worth it. Our lack of purpose would wear us down.

There is no doubt; we are called to follow Christ. But for what purpose? Jesus said to His disciples, "Follow me, and I will make you fishers of men." In other words, follow Christ with a purpose, and when the opportunity arises, execute that purpose. When we follow for no reason, we wear ourselves down. Too often, I encounter Christians who have run out of steam on the Christian journey. One person described it as boredom, the root of which I think is following without a purpose to pursue.

I feel that I understand better than most what it means to be a follower. I follow criminals for fifty hours a week and spend another ten hours watching crimes occur, making arrests, interviewing offenders, and writing reports. Following pays off. The reason we are on to these criminals is that most of them have avoided detection by patrol officers. I love following people, and I try to get better at it every day. Following is essential, and I spend more time doing it than anything else during the course of a week. When people ask what I do for a living, I tell them I watch criminals commit crimes. However, without having any purpose, surveillance would wear me down.

There comes a time when we all must stop simply following and get on to what we are made for. Do you remember when Jesus told His disciples that where He was going, they could not follow? Peter was overwhelmed and asked, "Lord, why can I not follow you now? I will lay down my life for you" (John 13:37). And Peter would do just that; he would ultimately die for his testimony of Christ. But Peter needed to stop following and start leading, and his leadership brought many thousands to Christ.

I believe Jesus would say the same to us:

Follow me, and I will show you what you must do. When you discover your purpose, do it. Don't look back and do not worry at all. I will be there with you. I will guide you when you are unsure of where to go. I will declare to you the mysteries of God, and you will know me better. I will help you in every way.

So, do you have a sense of purpose? Is there anything in your life that makes following Christ worth your time?

Experience Counts for Something

"If any of you lacks wisdom, let him ask God, who gives generously to all without reproach, and it will be given him" (James 1:5)

I once had a relatively new officer ride along with me for a week while I was on duty. I drive an unmarked vehicle, undercover, yet still function as a duly sworn police officer. My experiences and exposure are much different than those in uniform. The officer had been on the department for just two years. He was very young and looked even younger. Two years on a busy police department is just enough time to get a sense of the job and gain a few repetitions in dealing with crises.

One of the more obvious distinctions between my assignment and a patrol officer's assignment is exposure. A patrol officer is seen before he sees. A patrol car can be spotted by a suspicious person almost immediately. Suspicious people have time to react, to hide if necessary when a patrol car comes down the street. As a detective in an unmarked car, I can go into neighborhoods undetected. When parked in a subtle location, I can observe the natural flow and movement of the area. Oftentimes, I can be found in areas where crime is occurring right in front of me.

By having exposure to people in their natural element, it becomes rather easy to predict their behavior; they are just being themselves, doing what they want to do. With enough time on the streets, undercover detectives often find themselves in the right place at the right time to see the right things. This is not luck, but experience and a great deal of specialized training. The young police officer had never seen anything like this before. He was amazed at what the community looked like through the lens of an officer not seen by criminals as they went about their business.

I have discovered, however, that bringing the inexperienced into this arena is a huge responsibility, and in this instance, it almost proved to be fatal. We were following a group of young men in a stolen vehicle who had just committed a residential burglary. The suspects were heavily armed with handguns, and I was coordinating an intercept by our tactical units. This is the safest way to apprehend and arrest dangerous criminals.

The officers on our tactical detail are highly trained professionals and are excellent at what they do. In my world, I see this type of dynamic situation unfold almost every day.

As the tactical officers moved into position on the suspect's car, one of the occupants sensed that the vehicles around them were cops (he was correct). He told the driver to make a quick right turn into a cul-de-sac. The passengers jumped out and started to run while the driver turned around and fled. I was traveling behind the pack of tactical officers, so as the suspect vehicle veered off, the tactical officers bypassed them. This left me stopped in traffic at the mouth of the cul-de-sac, and I could see the suspects fleeing their vehicle.

One of the occupants was running in our direction and was quickly approaching us. He pulled out a gun from his jacket pocket and was looking around for a place to toss it. The young officer in my car forgot that he was in an unmarked police vehicle. Before I could say anything, he opened his door, drew his weapon, and yelled for the suspect to drop the gun. It turned out that the suspect was a juvenile, a fifteen-year-old boy. The boy saw us and turned and ran. I yelled to the young officer to get back into the car, and since we now had been exposed, we had to take action.

By this time, our tactical officers had made a quick U-turn and were entering the cul-de-sac. These officers carry advanced weapons, both lethal and non-lethal. They have the means and the experience to handle just about any situation effectively, and usually without any injuries. There were approximately twenty tactical officers around us, yet the young officer, having no undercover experience, acted and almost shot the boy.

The boy with the gun was scared. If the young officer had stayed concealed in our car, we would have been able to watch him toss the gun (and us retrieve it) and coordinate by radio his movement to the tactical officers. Fortunately, the boy just turned and ran, buying us some time to adjust and improvise. In the end, everybody was arrested without injuries to occupants and police officers.

Reviewing the incident reveals that the young officer, though having two years of experience as a police officer, did not evaluate his situation, and he lacked discernment. He could not distinguish between being a uniformed officer and an undercover officer. Standard procedure would have been to alert the tactical officers that the boy was armed and let them handle the situation. That is why we called in the tactical units—to minimize the risk of injury or death to both the suspects and police.

Discernment is essentially reasoned knowledge. Wisdom, therefore, is applied knowledge. Discernment is the key to wise living, and wise living is the key to spiritual manhood. We are capable of thinking before we respond. Ultimately, that is the difference between reacting and responding, what we think first. James, the brother of Jesus, wrote to encourage the believers who were experiencing difficulties through persecution. "Count it all joy when you meet trials of various kinds" (James 1:2). He understood that endurance begins with a proper perspective. Trials are necessary for the making of a man. However, if one does not have a proper perspective, he cannot make proper decisions.

Understanding this, James wrote to encourage the believers. There would be some who could not understand what James was writing about. How can we consider it joy when we experience difficulties? How can the believer get to the place where this happens? All of us fail trials from time to time, some more often than others. Knowing this, James wrote that we should ask God for His perspective on the trials we face in our lives. "If any of you lacks wisdom, let him ask God, who gives generously to all without reproach, and it will be given him" (James 1:5). How does God answer?

Does God explain the trials that we face? No. God simply reveals Himself. And when we look at Him seeking to understand, we see a God who knows all things. He only allows into our lives things He approves. He is able to keep us from anything else. When we face trials, every circumstance has been sifted through God's fingers before they touch our lives. Not only that, but He also already knows how we will respond. If God knows we lack the wisdom for a mature response, what do you think He should do about that? Should He protect us from more trials or bring more to help us?

God gives us a healthy perspective on how to get through trials and difficulties. By seeking God's perspective, we gain discernment. When we apply that perspective, we gain wisdom. The beauty of discernment is that we can carry it with us for the rest of our life, into any other trials we face. This process is how we grow up and become mature Christians.

193

Without discernment, wisdom is not gained, and without trials, discernment is not shaped.

Wanting More, Getting Less

But the people refused to obey the voice of Samuel. And they said, "No! But there shall be a king over us, that we also may be like all the nations, and that our king may judge us and go out before us and fight our battles" (1 Samuel 8:19-20)

It is challenging, when reading through the history of the people of Israel in the Old Testament, to find a good leader who led the people consistently throughout his leadership term. Prophets, judges, and kings were called by God to lead the people, but history does not speak favorably of the people's resolve to obey God and worship Him alone. Some of the most famous leaders in the archives of Jewish history have some stains on their leadership resumes. Only a few mentioned throughout Old Testament history have consistently good leadership records. Samuel is one of the leaders with a consistent, unblemished record.

Samuel became a leader to the nation before they had kings, during the period of the judges. His mother dedicated him to the service of the Lord when he was a child. A man named Eli mentored him. Scripture notes, "Samuel grew, and the Lord was with him and let none of his words fall to the ground" (I Samuel 3:19). The Lord's presence was with Samuel, and everything he said under God's direction came true. Samuel was a prophet of God, and God revealed His word directly through him.

Israel was to be a nation set apart from all other nations. They were to be a Theocracy, a government under the authority of God. God directed leaders to guide the people to be obedient to Him and His word. Leaders were to be His servants, leading the people as He saw fit, whether strengthening them in times of conflict or nurturing them in times of peace. Essentially, everything was to be directed by the Lord, and the Lord would bless the people, providing peace and prosperity for them.

If the people obeyed the Lord, they would have peace in the land in which they lived, their fields would be bountiful, and their reputation among the nations would be respected. But the people were rebellious, each one doing as they saw fit in their eyes, and not the Lord's. They were not interested in a Theocracy, as God had prescribed to them. They wanted what all the other nations had, a king. Kings represented authority and power.

The elders came to Samuel when he was old, knowing he would not lead much longer. They realized his sons were not capable of leading in Samuel's place. So, they asked that Samuel appoint a king for the nation. Samuel must have wondered what he could have done better to demonstrate to the people that they were distinct from other nations. Samuel knew that once they went this route, they could not go back. Samuel was displeased by their request (8:6). But, after seeking the Lord, he was instructed to select a king for the people. The Lord said, "obey the voice of the people in all that they say to you, for they have not rejected you, but they have rejected me from being king over them" (8:7).

So, under God's direction, Samuel appointed a king. However, before doing so, he warned the people what their decision would bring. When a king reigns, he takes all that the people have. Samuel lays this out in verses 11-17, stating the king will enslave their sons and daughters, take their finest crops, and impose heavy taxes. In fact, their third king, Solomon, taxed the people so severely that the nation divided over the issue and was never united again.

The people wanted more by appointing a king, but they received so much less. Isn't that typical? We tend to want what others have because we think they have it better than us. The people of Israel had it best, and they lost that perspective. It seems that historically, their struggle was endurance. They got bored with what they had, looked at what others had, and pursued it. I appreciate that God warned the people before He gave them what they were asking for, but I wonder why God gives us what we shouldn't have.

Can you think of a time that you prayed for something you wanted, like a new job, but once you got the job you hated it? Does that mean God gave you something that He knew would be bad for you because you wanted it? Or maybe, did God want you to experience a test of contentment through difficult circumstances and used the new job you desired to do so? Why does God answer our prayers? Why would He give us something that makes things worse for us?

Perhaps God gives us the desires of our heart, even when we desire what is not healthy for us. The people of Israel wanted a king, so they could have what all the other nations had. God gave the people a king who was a warrior and stood a head taller than all others. This satisfied the people of Israel. But from this point on, the Jewish people would rise and fall by the king who was in power.

Saul was their first king. He reigned for forty years over the nation. He was a bad king, and God intervened. He could have ended the role of king after Saul, telling the people that the experiment was not successful. He could have made an example out of him. However, God chose to end Saul's heritage to prevent anyone from his family line from being king after him. Then, God had Samuel (the one the people had rejected) go out and find the king who would establish an everlasting line of kings, David.

Why did God choose Saul as king over Jesse, David's father? God chose both Saul and David, so both were chosen for a reason. What would be a good reason for God to appoint Saul as king over the people of Israel? Perhaps it is easier to contemplate the question from a modern perspective: Why would God give me the desires of my heart if my desires are not healthy? After reading this story, it is impossible to conclude that God is not involved in giving things to His children that are not good for them.

I believe in a good God who loves me beyond comprehension and knows me better than I know myself. I also believe it is His nature to desire what is best for me. I have read in numerous passages in the Old Testament that God is a jealous God. He wants His creation to seek Him first. I also understand that He will not compete with the desires of our hearts. But He wants us to be fully His. The only conclusion I can draw is that God wants us to reject the things we once desired and pursue only what is according to His will.

Rightest Decisions

"I am the Lord your God, who teaches you to profit, who leads you in the way you should go" (Isaiah 48:17b)

How often do you find yourself in a situation where you do not know what to do? Your life probably has enough of a routine that most of what you experience in a given day is predictable and does not leave you wondering what to do. Rarely are you suddenly caught up in a situation that draws you in unprepared. But I realize there are some occupations (and marriages) that just keep throwing variables in one's direction. And these variables can make it difficult to breathe at times. However, if you are in that environment, you expect turbulence, even though you may not enjoy it.

Rightest is an adjective that is not often used. It is defined as following what is good, proper, or just: right conduct. So, the challenge in every situation is to do the rightest thing at that moment. If you work in a high-stress, fast-paced environment, challenges come on quickly. Consider the pressure of those who work on Wall Street, in the pit. That's a high-stress environment, but are they swept away by the stress? No. They work through it, doing their job. After a tough day or a down day, they get some rest, then go right back to it the next day. They expect their job to carry stress with it. With experience, they develop a sense of the rightest thing they should do to meet a particular challenge.

Annually, our police department requires that we pass three scenarios in our simulator training. We stand in front of a screen holding a specially made gun that fires laser strikes at our target. Before each scenario begins, we are told what we have walked into. For example, we may be in a building where the alarm is going off. Given that information, the scenario begins. The officer is expected to respond to what may happen next. Suppose a man suddenly comes around the corner. Is he the owner of the building checking on the alarm or a burglar who broke in? What is he holding? Is he armed? Whatever happens next is uncertain; however, each officer must be certain in his response to it.

These scenarios are not designed to trick the officer, but to expose him to uncertainties. The training is designed to evaluate decision-making skills. Why did the officer shoot? Why didn't he? Did he observe the second person hiding around the corner? Did he panic or get flustered? Why is this training necessary for police officers who are making the same critical decisions all day, every day on the streets? I think the answer is obvious: citizens want some assurance that police officers are capable of making the right decision every single time.

I have learned something in Christian living: every situation we encounter can be faced with an appropriate response. How can I be so confident in this? Well, it is God's nature to lead us in the way we should go. Our lives have three components: training, responding, and correcting. Every day, throughout the day, all day, one of these three components is happening in your life. Sometimes, they are combined in your scenario, but they are always at work.

Training is preparation for a proper response, designed to teach a particular skill or behavior. In sports, training is designed to enhance performance. Those who do not train hard do not perform well. In policing, training simulates real life, refines fine motor skills, and identifies areas needed for improvement. All training must include some degree of correcting. The goal of training is to respond appropriately to every real-life situation. If all of life is training, and none of it is responding, something is wrong. Your profession is no different; neither is your marriage. Without training, we cannot expect to have an appropriate response to what comes our way. God is relational and always at work, providing us training in life so we can apply an appropriate response to everything.

Responding is a reaction to something. When training, we learn to consider appropriate responses so the right decision can be made every time. For police officers, I doubt many would debate the high volume of critical decisions they have to make every day. How much grace does society give police officers for getting it wrong? One bad choice may lead to devastating consequences. There is little or no room for error. If police officers are expected to make the right decision every single time on every single call for service, under a time restraint, pressure, and scrutiny, is it reasonable to think each of us, in our own world, could do the same?

For example, let's say you and your wife are angry with each other. You each had a bad day and wore each other down. You both made some bad decisions. There is now some resentment that has worked its way into your marriage. The day has come to an end, and you lay in bed, frustrated. When you consider what to do next, do you have any options? Is one option better than the other? How did these options come to you? Do you believe in a God who leads you in the way you should go? Are you capable of doing the rightest thing and letting go of the results? I am sure you are capable. However, the more you train for this, the better or more consistent your response will be. Responding is not reacting because responses are calculated. When you get really good at training, you can rely on your reactions to be more like quick responses. Perhaps that is why police officers are not called "first reactors."

Correcting is putting something right. Sometimes, we just do not do the right thing. Every time I work on a home project, this is the case for me. I do every home improvement project at least twice. The first time it is always done wrong. I tend not to like reading directions, or at least not all of them. Leaving a job as the mess I created is not an option. It's funny how much time one project takes when it must be done more than once. Correction takes time. When it comes to my marriage, the same is true. To put something right in my marriage, I must put time into it—as much time as required because the option I chose the first time was a bad one. Bad choices tend to lead to bad problems. Bad problems cannot be fixed without making good choices. Do you believe in a God who shows you how to correct problems and put them right? The time it takes to put things right is sometimes the most judicious use of time.

In what area(s) of your life are you in training? Do you see the need for additional training? Do you accept the bad decisions that you make? Can you tell when you made a bad decision? How does God lead you in the way you should go? He promises to do this for you but notice one important word in our verse: should. When you do what you should not do, expect correction. God will not make you do something you do not want to do, but He may correct you until you do it right. You can make the rightest decisions.

On Mercy

"It depends not on human will or exertion, but on God, who has mercy" (Romans 9:16)

Why do we, as humans, struggle to accept God's mercy as the only means for salvation? Where grace is receiving something we do not deserve, is mercy the withholding of punishment we do deserve? If we accept that God is holy and perfect and that we are not, then we must conclude that if He judges, His righteous standard is a fair scale for justice. But do we want God to be fair? I, for one, do not. I need Him to show me mercy.

We live in a society where the rule of law must be upheld. For every crime, there is a subsequent punishment. It is reasonable to expect that law enforcement personnel, from officers to prosecutors, uphold the laws and enforce them justly. Punishment, however, is somewhat arbitrary. A first-time offender gets a lesser sentence than a repeat offender. We generally accept that a first-time offender deserves a lesser punishment than a repeat offender. We acknowledge that this principle is reasonable and expect judges to show mercy to first-timers.

For four and a half years, I was a detective for our Repeat Offender Program. The program's goal was to identify offenders who were career criminals committing felony offenses, apprehend them in a new crime, and enter them into the program as Repeat Offenders. We had a red stamp that said: "Repeat Offender," that we stamped on the booking paperwork. This label would ensure that the case would go to the Repeat Offender division at the County Attorney's office. A criminal identified as a repeat offender was subject to harsher sentencing after conviction in a criminal case.

I received phone calls all day and night after criminals were arrested. The arresting officers knew this program's effectiveness in assuring that the perpetrator received a just punishment for their crime. Most did not qualify as a Repeat Offender, and their case would go through the system as usual. However, there were times when an officer caught a bonified Repeat Offender. These suspects had multiple prior felony convictions and were usually on probation or parole, on drugs, or were unemployed. In these cases, I would respond and interview the offender.

If the suspect qualified as a Repeat Offender, their booking paperwork was stamped. From that point on, the entire justice system was designed to show no mercy. The Repeat Offender would be charged with the highest offense applicable without an opportunity to plead to a lesser charge. The only chance a criminal had for a lesser sentence was to take the plea deal to their charge rather than taking the case to trial. Trial sentences were always harsher than plea deals.

After a conviction, I would receive a subpoena to appear in court to testify on behalf of the state at the sentencing hearing. It was my responsibility to explain why this person was a Repeat Offender and why I believed this person would re-offend upon release. Sentencing hearings have two sides to them: an aggravation hearing and a mitigation hearing. The prosecutor presents the aggravation hearing to enhance punishment. The defense then mounts a mitigation hearing to lessen the sentence for the offender. But defense attorneys knew their client's Repeat Offender designation crippled them. They could not dispute the salient characteristics of a Repeat Offender since these factors were well documented.

Nonetheless, regardless of the label, every convicted felon did the same thing at the sentencing hearing: he or she asked for mercy. It was the only thing they could hope for. However, I never witnessed one person deny their label as a Repeat Offender. At sentencing, not one criminal ever said they did not deserve punishment for their crime. They all accepted their fate and recognized that the judge had the final word on their length of sentence. Though painful at times to admit, every offender knew they got what they deserved.

I have learned that, according to God's holy standard, I am a Repeat Offender. Every offense I have committed is worthy of a death sentence. There are no misdemeanors in heaven. God's judgment of me would be appropriate, and my punishment deserved. My offenses are well known to Him, and the prosecutor in my case is the devil himself. The devil stands before God and makes the case that I deserve the death penalty (Revelation 12:10). Then, Jesus Christ mounts my defense. He tells the Judge that my offenses are worthy of the death penalty, but that by His blood, He has already accepted punishment on my behalf. The Judge acknowledges that my transgressions are worthy of death. He agrees to the substitutionary death sentence already carried out by Jesus and tells me my punishment is paid in full.

God then blots out the stamp labeling me as a Repeat Offender and considers me righteous. I am righteous because the Judge sees Christ in me, and His righteousness has become my righteousness. I will not have to go through the court system ever again, though I sometimes re-offend. This is mercy. Is it fair? Yes. If every offense deserves a just punishment, then it is fair because Jesus took the punishment on my behalf. Jesus is a fantastic defense attorney if you ever need one. When He argues our case, He always accepts the punishment on our behalf, and the Judge has ruled that His punishment stands in our place and is acceptable. If only we all knew that we need to Lawyer up.

The Biggest Obstacle to Love is Not Hate, But Avoidance, Part 1

And he (Jesus) said to them, "Which of you who has a friend will go to him at midnight and say to him, 'Friend, lend me three loaves, for a friend of mine has arrived on a journey, and I have nothing to set before him'; and he will answer from within, 'Do not bother me; the door is now shut, and my children are with me in bed. I cannot get up and give you anything'?" (Luke 11:5-7)

While at work one day preparing to serve a search warrant at a residence, the officers I was with, and I heard a man and woman calling for our help about thirty yards away. The man yelled, "This lady has been stabbed!" We kept a few men back at the residence and hurried to the woman who was slumped over and holding her stomach. As we approached, the man helping her pointed across the street and said, "That guy over there is stabbing someone!" We looked across the street and saw a man standing over and repeatedly stabbing another man who was on the ground.

As I stayed with the woman, five police officers ran directly toward the two across the street. All five of them were so locked onto the stabbing incident that they failed to notice the car driving at over forty miles an hour right at them. With no regard for their own safety, they did not pause. The car just missed striking all five of the officers simultaneously. As they were approaching, the assailant looked up, stood over the wounded man, and surrendered. Though the victim was in grave condition, the officers had saved his life.

The two stabbing victims lived together and were leaving their apartment. The assailant, who lived next door, followed and attacked them, still angry over a dispute they had earlier in the day. So, who were neighbors to the couple? Though the couple's attacker lived next door, clearly, he was not their neighbor. The policemen were neighbors to a man and woman they had never met before.

At the time of this incident, we were all busy with a pressing matter to deal with. However, when the man called out, the need appeared to be urgent, and our response seemed necessary. Initially, we had no idea of the gravity of the situation. But isn't that often the way it is? We tend to avoid situations that may draw us into bigger problems. By avoiding the small interruptions, we avoid the major ones. Though this may be an extreme example, consider all the little ways our view of who our neighbors are might arise.

Consider walking along a sidewalk and seeing three people coming in your direction who appear to be up to no good. What would you do? Many would move to the other side of the street to avoid them or turn down a different street altogether. Sometimes, it may be sensible to avoid people out of fear, whether for a good cause or not. But we also often avoid people who are different or disagree with us, whether culturally, ideologically, or even theologically.   In some cases, we avoid people out of convenience because they may take some of our time. And sadly, we might avoid people who are suffering because we feel we cannot find an appropriate way to help.

Take a look at the story of the Good Samaritan in Luke 10. When the priest and the Levite saw the man in need, what did they do? They passed by on the other side; they avoided the man on the road, who had been stripped, beaten, and left half dead. These two men concluded that the man would be better off dead than helped by them. But when the Samaritan came along the beaten man, he stopped and helped. This story was told by Jesus after a lawyer had asked, "who is my neighbor?" While Jesus allowed him to answer his own question with this parable, in a sense, He flipped the question around to be, "Who is not my neighbor?" Far too often, we pass by some to get to the people we want to be around. Sure, we are neighborly with these people, but it is those we pass by who determine our concept of what a neighbor is.

Often, I see this in churches; people tend to avoid those they disagree with. Sometimes, people leave churches because they disagree with others in the church. It is easier for many to avoid people they disagree with than to meet with them. I have met few people who are willing to invite people into their lives whom they disagree with. I have found few leaders who bring individuals into their inner circle who may disagree with them.

How many people have we seen ignored or avoided because they are difficult to deal with? While it is understandable to bypass people we disagree with, it counters the command to love. If God's love has had its effect on us, it must transform us into people who seek others, including those we do not like or who do not like us. We must be willing to be vulnerable to them as a discipline of love. We must allow God's love working through us to work through challenging relationships.

Perhaps a good measure of how we love should be based on the extent that we invite people into our lives who disagree with us or are different than us. Maybe this gracious expression is the difference between those who love their neighbors and those who do not.

I confess I was once the pastor who had no patience with difficult people. I thought I was right in every relationship and found a way to be too busy for burdensome people. I avoided a lot of people to reach those I wanted to be around. I tried to persuade people to think like me, not to help them, but to make it easier for me to be around them. Law enforcement has taught me how to approach people in need and to see their needs more clearly. I have discovered who I want to be around—those in need. I did not learn this in the church; in fact, I believe avoidance culture is often acceptable in the church. I have often felt like an outsider at church. Perhaps that has helped me seek the hurting, the neglected, and the avoided. The discipline of "who is my neighbor?" is to ensure that we do not disregard difficult members of our congregation by avoiding them.

Who is not my neighbor? Well, every person we would rather avoid than be with is treated as though they are not our neighbor. Let's ask ourselves the following questions: Do I attend my chosen church because I agree with everything that is said or taught? Do I live in a neighborhood because everyone around me is like me? Do I work around people who share the same convictions I have? If our answer to each question is yes, then we must ask ourselves, what measure of love is that? Perhaps, the most accurate measure of love we have for our neighbors is the extent to which we surround ourselves with people not like us.

Who is my neighbor? Like the Samaritan, neighbors are those we go to. When we get to them, we must assess what they need, no matter how inconvenient it may be. Then, we hold tight, standing firm, not for glory or admiration, but devotion. We can't pass by, nor avoid them. Sure, life would be easier if we did. We could surround ourselves with people that admire us and think as we do. We may be able to accomplish much by keeping those in our inner circle on our page. However, a lot of our neighbors will be passed by. So, ask yourself, would I rather spend time with my neighbor?

The Biggest Obstacle to Love is Not Hate, But Avoidance, Part 2

"But I say to you who hear, Love your enemies, do good to those who hate you, bless those who curse you, pray for those who abuse you" (Luke 6:27-28)

We are living in a time when many people hate the police. As I write this, assaults on police officers are on the rise. During my career, I have experienced the most extreme form of abuse having been shot at. The rifle round fired at me missed my head by four inches. I have also been spat on, kicked, punched, and called every name in the urban dictionary. I have been sued half a dozen times by people trying to capitalize on society's diminishing view of police conduct. I have learned that it has never been personal. These assaults happened to me because of proximity. I came into a problem; I went to them. Their actions were not really against me but toward what I represent. Their attacks were against those in authority, acting on behalf of the city to bring peace and protection. I have never met a police officer who, after incurring abuse on a call, refused to do it again. They just keep doing their job.

Looking at the verse above, Jesus reinforced a valuable lesson about love when He spoke to the crowds. There are four aspects of His statement to unpack here. First, Jesus commands His listeners to love their enemies. Note the importance of proximity here; he is instructing them to become vulnerable, exposed, close in distance. By telling the listeners to love, he is explicitly commanding them to welcome, to entertain, to be kind to, to love dearly. In other words, do something with them, for them, and out of fondness for them. Is this possible for us? It is if we want to love our enemies.

Second, Jesus tells the listeners to do good to those who hate them. If we do good to those who hate us, will they receive our gesture as kindness and goodness? Probably not. But as followers of Christ, we are called to love at a higher level. Much that we do will be mocked, criticized, and overlooked, and if we expect something in return, it will be impossible to sustain our efforts.

Moreover, doing good to our enemies requires us to get close, to get behind enemy lines. We need to strive for access relentlessly, penetrating the established walls that are intended to keep us out. Now, it is essential to remember that Jesus never promised that this kind of love is the key to reconciliation with those who hate us. Likewise, He never promised we would get positive results for our efforts. Because of this, how many times have we found ourselves justifying why it is useless to try? But as followers of Christ, we must continue drawing from the well to love, to do good to others, even if the water poured out seems wasted. We must trust that if Jesus commands this kind of love, it is never a waste.

Third, Jesus tells the listeners to bless those who curse them. How often do we tend to pray for those who hate us? Likely, not very often, if at all. And if we do, it may be self-serving, praying that they get what they deserve, that they would stop hating, or that they may begin to see things our way. But Jesus said we must pray a blessing on them. So, what should we pray, and how should that prayer sound? Well, bless them when you pray to the Father in heaven and bless them to their face. Recently, a friend told me about a problematic neighbor he once had and the ongoing battle the two of them endured for years. I asked how the problem was resolved? He said the neighbor finally moved. Did that really fix the problem? No, all that did was make things easier for my friend. As I read through Christ's words to His listeners, I do not sense that ease is the goal, nor the end result. If ease comes, may it only arise because God's love working through us penetrated the heart of another, and brought about redemption and reconciliation.

Finally, Jesus asks us to pray, implying this kind of love may incur abuse from those we are called to love. They may curse you, mock you, and even abuse you. They may act aggressively against you. They may start rumors about you, trying to hurt you. This is where the power of God working through the follower of Christ must be applied. As Christians, we must learn to be unoffendable. It is a discipline that we must master. It is a choice, a decision that must be made over and over again. Undoubtedly, we will all be tempted; "You don't deserve this. You don't need to take this." These are the enemy's lies intended to keep us off the track of being neighborly. Why do so many in our society think the church is filled with judgmental people? Perhaps it is because so many people have been dealing with judgmental neighbors that leave the neighborhood behind to head to church every Sunday.

In talking with a church leader, I asked him how he deals with people who do not like him. His response was staggering. He said, "I don't think I know of anybody who doesn't like me." How is this possible? I do not think any of us need to journey very far away from our safety zone to get exposed to resistance. I fear that too many avoid their enemies, so all can like them. I was fortunate to enter into a career where I had to figure this out. Police officers must continually expose themselves to hostilities almost daily. They accept the threats and hazards that come with the job and expect their training and experience to get them through even the harshest interactions.

I believe policing has two significant challenges. The first is to never give up and always answer the call. With little information to go by, they head toward danger. Occasionally, people run, and police give chase. It is fun; I will not deny it. It is fun chasing someone who is trying to get away. I don't blame them. They know what is going to happen if they get caught. Over all the years of doing this job, I can only think of a few times when the fleeing felon got away and avoided arrest. It would shock nobody if I said this job has many occupational hazards. Most of us have suffered injuries during our careers; some have made the ultimate sacrifice. I thank God that He has invited me into this world, where officers never, ever give up, no matter the cost.

The second challenge is much different from the first. I believe that police should master the art of confession. To develop this skill, police must make some conclusions. First, no matter what happened prior to handcuffing a prisoner, police officers have nothing to prove to a person in handcuffs. But cops are humans with emotions, and it is in these moments that we must exercise restraint. Too often, here is where police officers get into trouble as they take a cheap shot at a handcuffed prisoner. There is no reason for this, and nothing is gained.

Furthermore, we must begin a process of working the prisoner into a confession. We must not lead them to think of themselves as the bad guys and us as the good guys. We must learn to become relatable, even toward the most dangerous or deviant people. We must not call them names or treat them as they may deserve.

During my career, I confess that I have never been the most tactical officer in the department. I am not the best shooter, I am not the strongest nor the fastest, and I will never be good enough to make it on a SWAT team. However, I believe I may be one of the best interviewers and interrogators in the department. I attribute much of this to my Christian convictions, to do good even to those who do evil against me. Some think the Christian is gullible, naïve, and falls for whatever they are told. Perhaps that is true with some. However, with training and experience in detecting deception, police officers can learn the art of empathy, even toward the hardest and the harshest of criminals. I admit, sometimes I need to be a performer to do this well. Sometimes, I am angry or hurt. But I believe this must be put aside to accomplish what must come from my interaction with the defendant: the confession.

In the same way, to do good to those who abuse us may require that we conceal how we may be feeling. To some extent, it is a performance that allows us to do what is right despite how we may feel. Perhaps sometimes it is theatrical, but maybe this skill will become conditioned into everyday practice, and we will begin to have genuine empathy for those who abuse us.

What is the point here? As I said at the beginning, the biggest obstacle to love is not hate but avoidance. Proximity exposes our character in ways avoidance never can. It is insincere to say we love all when we avoid most. Much like police officers who make a living determining the balance between the pursuit of conflict and creating safe distances, Christians must engage with those who do not want to be loved by us. It is never acceptable to conclude that if a person does not want to be around us, then we won't be around them. We must master the art of the pursuit of love. Move-in close to those who love you—there is nothing wrong with that. But just as importantly, move in close with those who do not want to be loved by you. Move-in close to your enemies, to those who hate you, and do good to them. Move-in close to those who curse you and what you believe. Close the gap to those who have hurt you. Not so close that they can abuse you, but where they can see you from a safe distance while you're still close enough to love them. This kind of love is not for your benefit but for His glory.

"And who is my neighbor?" Do you remember who it was that asked Jesus this question? It was a lawyer seeking to justify himself (Luke 10:29). He was a man who avoided those he did not want to love. In his profession, people came to him when they had a problem. Once hired, he felt justified in providing his services to those who came to him. But Jesus's words taught the lawyer that his capacity to love was not measured by how many people came to him. Instead, love was his response to anyone in need. Applying this today, even an enemy can be our neighbor.

Two is One, and One is None

"If you keep my commandments, you will abide in my love, just as I have kept my Father's commandments and abide in his love." (John 15:10)

Obedience is an essential characteristic of those who are to be disciples of Christ. Yet, I find it interesting that as soon as obedience is discussed in the Church, many tend to gravitate toward moral obedience rather than missional obedience. In other words, people tend to believe that good clean living is an obedient Christian life. Missional obedience is rarely given significant consideration when we contemplate what exactly Christ has called us to do. Which of these did Jesus have in mind when he told his disciples, "If you keep my commandments, you will abide in my love"?

Moral obedience is proper and good. However, it can lead to two extremes: asceticism (severe self-discipline and avoidance of all forms of indulgence) or self-righteousness (being convinced of one's virtue, especially in contrast to the actions and beliefs of others). Though these are extreme applications regarding what it means to live a moral life, those who believe obedience is measured by morality will be vulnerable to either. Yet neither of these two endpoints is healthy for spiritual people. It is possible to be very moral yet to be spiritually dead.

Missional obedience is living on a mission with God in obedience to the Holy Spirit. It is demonstrating in tangible actions and declaring in creative ways the gospel of Jesus Christ to others. This type of missional work is best expressed through fellowship. The Spirit of God unites the Body of Christ as a persuasive or powerful force that's on display in a community for others to witness.

The backdrop for John 15:10 finds Jesus just having finished dinner with the 11 disciples. Judas was already on his way to betray Jesus by reporting His location and leading an arrest team to where He could be found. Judas must have known the plan; that Jesus would be getting up from the dinner table and leaving to go to the garden to the east of the temple in Jerusalem. When Judas left Jesus, they were all still sitting in the house together. Once Judas left them, the rest got up to head for the garden. It was then that Jesus began to speak his deep and intense final words to his disciples.

Walking with the disciples, Jesus said to them, "If you keep my commandments, you will abide in my love." He compares his obedience to what he is telling them, "just as I have kept my Father's commandments and abide in his love." Since moral obedience was not Jesus' challenge in this world, he must have been referring to missional obedience. Consider how many times we read in the Gospels where Jesus said he came to do his Father's will, or that he did nothing unless it was given to him by his Father. Time and time again, Jesus reiterated this to his disciples.

The spiritual obey Christ by doing the work given to them, in obedience to the working of the Holy Spirit in their life. The spiritual listen to the voice of God, the whisper in their soul, and respond. Keep in mind that missional work is expressed through community living. God calls us to one another; to live and to love, to give and to sacrifice, to bless and to forgive. The spiritual are not the ones they were called to be unless they are living within a community committed to these virtues and values.

Of all the tools I use in law enforcement in the performance of my duties, the one that makes me most nervous is my flashlight. I am not a second or third-shift patrol officer who uses a flashlight every day, but when I need it, I really need it. I often work through the day and into the night. Since flashlights operate off a battery, their usefulness is contingent on being charged. Depending on the amount of time needed on any application, a flashlight may be necessary for thirty seconds or thirty minutes. Police officers often remind one another with a saying about flashlights, "two is one, and one is none." It is good practice always to have a secondary flashlight available that you can rely on if your primary light goes out. Any officer who had not practiced this discipline and lost their essential light at just the wrong time would share my nervousness about this.

Likewise, missional work cannot be achieved with only one source of light. Christ was telling his disciples to be joined together, abiding in Him, by also abiding in one another, combining the source of light in each other's life, so that the world would see and take notice. There are times when one's light may be weakened due to the lack of recharge in their battery. However, that person will continue to see because those around them are still projecting light. Perhaps, we need to be reminded that "two is one, and one is none." To abide in Christ by being united with one another is obedience if our intent is to project light. When isolated, we are at risk of a diminishing light source.

Going back to the beginning of Jesus's final conversation with his disciples in John 13, I searched for commands or imperatives made by Jesus to his disciples. The first command I found was right after Jesus washed the feet of his disciples. He turned and said, "you also ought to wash one another's feet" (13:14). Jesus reiterates his point immediately after that with another command, "you also should do just as I have done to you." After releasing Judas, he turned to his disciples and said, "A new commandment I give you, that you love one another: just as I have loved you, you also are to love one another" (13:34). Other than phrases such as "believe in me" and "abide in me," that's it. Up to this point in Jesus' discourse, the only commands he offers them is to live within a loving community, together, helping one another, remaining with one another.

Considering these seemingly simple commands, I ask myself, why do they seem so difficult to obey? In the 21st century church in America, how can we obey these commands if we change church communities continually for personal preference? Likewise, how are we to obey these commands if our churches merely offer up a one-hour production for spectators within the community? It is my conviction that we are sacrificing missional obedience for behavior modification—moral obedience. It seems that many today go to church to either feel better about themselves or to work on some unhealthy habits. Jesus had a far greater purpose for the church in mind when he taught his disciples just before his arrest. It is impossible to live the Spiritual Life without being dedicated to a Spiritual Community. Alone, we do not project light impressively. Together, our neighbors would not help but notice what the power of God can do when each light source unites. For this reason, I believe Jesus is teaching about missional obedience, not moral obedience.

The Spiritual Abide

"Abide in me, and I in you. As the branch cannot bear fruit in itself, unless it abides in the vine, neither can you, unless you abide in me. I am the vine; you are the branches. Whoever abides in me and I in him, he it is that bears much fruit, for apart from me you can do nothing" (John 15:4-5)

One of the most commonly discussed themes in modern theology is the question of what to do with "free will." This issue would be much easier to talk about and understand if the question were, "What should we do with our will?" The problem, I believe, in this discussion is that we have added the word "free." We assume it means we get to do what we want to do. We also assume that since God gave us a "free will," He is alright with how we navigate our lives. But I do not believe this is a biblical concept.

To explain, let's begin by considering the context of John 15:4-5. Jesus has only a short time left with His eleven remaining disciples; they will soon be leaving for the garden where Jesus will be arrested. Jesus was called by God to prepare these men to become apostles. As apostles, they would be uniquely endowed with gifts and the ability to demonstrate to the world that they were with Jesus. Then, they would be sent out by God to perform signs and miracles validating their calling. These men would be the original leading witnesses of Christ's resurrection. Jesus had kept them together during His earthly ministry. And now, in His final hours, He commanded them to love one another, to stick together, to take care of each other, as noted in John 13:34-35.

A few minutes later, Jesus assures the apostles that they will receive help from the Spirit of truth and that they will never be left alone (John 14:16-17). However, they would not be apostles on autopilot. Something was expected of them. Their work would not be completed in their own strength, nor by their own abilities. They would need to draw from the Source given to them from above. Their reward for drawing near would be incomprehensible peace, and they would bear much fruit for His Kingdom as a result.

Moving on to chapter 15, the first word in John 15:4 is abide. Abide is a translation of the Greek word *men'o*, a verb which means to stay (in a given place, state, relation, or expectancy), remain, continue, dwell, endure, be present, or stand. Jesus used this word ten times in the first ten verses of John 15. I believe this word, *men'o*, is at the heart of the question of "free will."

Assuming we do have a "free will" (and we do), this means we also have a choice. Do we stay, regardless of our circumstances, trials, hardships, pains, and difficulties, or do we walk away? The spiritual abide, whereas those caught up in worldly things, walk away. Though technically we are free to do so, what good is walking away if, by doing so, "you can do nothing" (v. 5)? The branch cannot bear fruit by itself. Jesus carried these eleven men through many miles and many lessons. They witnessed many miracles and learned about God's plan of salvation before any others, yet they still couldn't comprehend. It seems appropriate that Jesus would discuss the need for these men to abide in Him. At the time, I am sure they were all weighing the cost.

So, the question we must ask ourselves is this: Do we want to bear fruit, drawing the world to the Savior? If we don't want to do that because we are shy or embarrassed or unsure of what we might say when asked a hard question, we will just walk away from the vine and concern ourselves with ourselves. How is this a matter of "free will" if walking away bears no fruit? How can anyone suggest this is a good thing?

God gives each person a will, but let's not call it a free will. Without a will, there is no worship of God. What one does with that will can be their act of worship if they lay it aside and carry out the will of Christ. The Spiritual do what Jesus did—He put his will aside for the glory of His Father. The spiritual abide; they surrender their will, knowing Christ will never leave them, and they will produce much fruit. They do not live dormant or passive but boldly stand with the message of His resurrection to those who need a Savior.

When a person defines their will as a "free will," aren't they claiming sovereignty over their life? Isn't that person suggesting that God gave them the ability to navigate through their circumstances by their own intellect, desires, or interests? Consider, for example, offense. Do we get offended when we are cheated, harassed, or abused in any way? Why do we get offended? Isn't that a choice we have? Can we choose not to be offended? No doubt, we all have a right and are free to get offended. However, when we get offended, we are placing all the power into the offender's hands. How is that freedom? The offended becomes bound to the offender. Now, can you imagine what society would look like today if every person surrendered his or her right to offense and lived unoffendable? But to do so, we must forfeit that right, that "free will."

The next time you hear someone discuss 'free will' as God's gift to man, ask that person what good has ever come from that freedom? If you listen closely, you will hear that they credit themselves with all the good and decent things they have done. I am not suggesting they are not spiritual people; they very well may be. However, they may be misinformed on God's purpose in giving humanity a will in the first place. Suggest to that person that they forfeit that free will as though they no longer have it. See where the conversation goes from there.

Friendly Fire

"They will put you out of the synagogues. Indeed, the hour is coming when whoever kills you will think he is offering service to God" (John 16:2)

I moved to Arizona in 1995, shortly after a young man named Pat Tillman arrived to play football on a scholarship at Arizona State University. Tillman played at ASU from 1994-97 and is one of the most famous Sun Devil football players in history. He played with a rugged tenacity, seemingly present on nearly every tackle. During his college career, he was the Pac-10 Defensive Player of the Year, was a Second Team All-American, was named the 1997 Sun Bowl MVP, inducted into the Sun Bowl Hall of Fame, and named the 1997 Sporting News/Honda Scholar-Athlete of the Year.

Tillman was drafted by the Arizona Cardinals. The Bidwell family (owners of the team) understood the value he would bring to the team. They recognized the enthusiasm the community would have toward their draft pick. Tillman was exciting to watch and left everything he had on the field, never holding back in a single game. He played four seasons in the NFL with the Arizona Cardinals and would have played much longer had 9/11 not happened.

After that tragic day, Tillman passed up a contract extension, and in 2002 joined the United States Army and became a Ranger. His dedication to his country was no surprise to his fans, as they had witnessed the same commitment to his brothers on the football field. None would doubt he would bring the same tenacity to the war in Afghanistan. Tragically, he was killed in Afghanistan on April 22, 2004. Following his death, he was awarded a Purple Heart and a Silver Star by the United States Military. Tillman was posthumously honored with the NFL's Distinguished American Award in 2006.

However, an investigation concluded that Tillman was killed by friendly fire, and his death is still controversial. The tight grouping of rounds to his head may indicate that he was either shot from a close distance or was struck by a sniper. Many have speculated that his death may not have been accidental. Tillman was like a rock star among fellow soldiers. He was a member of the Army Rangers and a star professional football player.

He was admired by many of his fellow soldiers. Could this have aroused some jealousy? Tillman also outspokenly objected to the Iraq war and was an enthusiastic atheist. To those who were loyal to both military campaigns, might this have stirred hostility?

Maybe it's best if we just let this man and his legend rest in peace. We may never know all the answers behind his tragic death. However, the facts conclude that Pat Tillman was killed by someone in the US military. Was this an accidental ambush or an intentional attack as an act of betrayal? Tillman's death will likely be remembered as another great conspiracy theory to speculate. However, his death was not necessary. If he was struck by friendly fire, it was the result of two units on the same team misidentifying one another yet both engaging out of self-preservation. If he was attacked, though the rounds came from a US operator, he certainly did not die of friendly fire.

As Jesus prepared his disciples for their mission, to go into all the world making disciples, he commanded them to love one another to such a degree that 'all people will know that you are my disciples (John 13:35). Did this mean all people would love them back? Of course not. Though this kind of reciprocal love must be present among followers of Christ, it cannot be expected from outsiders. Jesus told his disciples that some people may hate them. The reason for their hate was directly related to the disciples' obedience to Christ's commands. In other words, the more Christians display their love for one another, the more some people will hate them.

The hatred Jesus was talking about should never come from inside His Church, the body of Christ. There is no excuse for that. If Jesus were to visit a church in the 21st Century, He would certainly know who is part of His Church and who isn't on any given Sunday. However, if you attend a Seeker-Sensitive congregation, could you observe those entering the building and distinguish who is Christian and who is not? Moreover, do you expect the same level of decorum from all in attendance? It does not require a huge leap of faith to assume that not all who come to church are Christian.

Suppose you attend church this weekend. You spend time meditating in worship and give sacrificially. You attentively engage in the sermon and then hang around the building connecting to others after service. Then, you are approached by a couple who tell you they have been watching you all hour. At first, you are honored that they have taken notice, but you quickly realize they are attacking you, intimidating you, harassing you, and mocking you. What would you do?

Jesus was preparing His disciples for this kind of conduct. He knew that in just a few weeks, after the great Day of Pentecost, the Holy Spirit would invade their hearts and give them courage and power to proclaim Christ in the synagogues. The synagogues are where the Jewish people gathered within their communities. The eleven remaining disciples were Jewish and had been connected to their religious community and their synagogues for their entire lives. Maybe they hoped that the Jewish people would embrace their message, the good news of Christ's resurrection.

However, the disciples would be hated, and not only by the world they were sent into to proclaim the Gospel but also in their hometowns and in their religious communities. But these men did not give up on the religious communities they grew up in. They went into them and tried to persuade people to believe. They were relentless, unashamed, and courageous. Perhaps, Jesus' words in John 16, having foreknowledge of this conflict, gave the disciples peace while taking on friendly fire.

Jesus tells the men, "They will put you out of the synagogues. Indeed, the hour is coming when whoever kills you will think he is offering service to God" (John 16:2). I will admit, that during my career in law enforcement, every offense committed against me in the performance of my duties, I have understood as the anticipated struggle in crime-fighting. I am prepared for it, I expect it, and I work with a team of men who also expect it and can handle whatever aggression may arise with competence and precision.

If we want to have seeker-sensitive congregations, should we not expect some of the same conflicts from within? I am not saying that there is anything wrong with opening the church doors to the non-believing community. I love that. But we are blurring the lines when our messages are more about behavior modification and less about the death and resurrection of Jesus Christ. If all we discuss is behavior issues in the church, nobody will ever take offense at that. But when the unbelieving world is confronted with the atoning blood of Christ on the cross, and the power of God to raise Him back to life to give us life, that will make people squirm. And if the majority of people in the church are squirming, then they will work together to oust you rather than collect their children and leave quietly.

Jesus did not hold back when telling the disciples the truth. Some would be killed by their own people, and they were told to expect resistance. We must reconcile that Jesus Christ is the dividing line within churches. Those of us who believe in Him must do the work we are called to do. But many of those who resist Him will fight against the work of the Holy Spirit, and the work of His followers. Here is a provoking question: would you continue to go to a church if you were one of the last followers of Christ doing the Lord's work He called you to do in His Church? An affirmative answer means you would risk taking on friendly fire, or worse, taking rounds from a church operator.

Life Through Christ

"In this the love of God was made manifest among us, that God sent His only Son into the world, so that we might live through him" (1 John 4:9)

The Gospel is the second chance we all need in life. With that said, most of us have burned through thousands of second chances and might wonder why another is available to us. As I reflect on this passage, many people come to mind. Some were arrested, strung out on heroin, their lives spiraling, and their prognosis bleak for a better future. It is heartbreaking to recall the number of times I have heard someone say, "Thank you for arresting me; this is my opportunity to get clean." I must admit, I really want to believe they will break free from addiction and get the fresh start they talk about. But experience tells me they will be back down this dark alley when they get the chance.

We often find ourselves making promises to God, vowing "to never do it again," and asking earnestly for a break from addiction, pain, or struggle. Though we are well aware that what we are doing is destructive, we just keep doing it. It's as though we are falling down a hill, unable to change directions or get a secure grip to stop the fall. These difficulties could be relational, financial, health-related, or a nasty vice that consumes us. If what you are reading does not relate to you, praise God—you have figured out a better way. However, if this describes you, it is you who is on my mind as I unfold what I notice in this verse.

As a new believer, I came into the faith with a drinking problem, yet I was only twenty years old. Though the desire for a life with Christ appealed to me, I was not comfortable with who I was sober, and was afraid to find out that I might not be likable. I came to Christ for salvation, but not for transformation. I continued drinking, not so much from addiction but out of fear of who I might be. It really wasn't an alcohol addiction but rather an identity complex. I could have been sober but did not want to be. I had a lot of guilt pounding on me, but I really did not try to break free. I knew the truth of forgiveness, redemption, and love, and was sure He loved me despite me. Desperate, my prayer life was simple: "God, please forgive me once again and do not harden my heart."

More than anything, I wanted a second chance, even though it seemed I had burned through at least one each day. I knew enough to understand that if I ever stopped caring about what I was doing, I would be consumed by my vices. I was afraid of callouses on my heart that would make me numb and cause me to give up. I was actually working against Christ living in me. He was always on my mind and would prompt me and remind me of who I am, and who He was. I never doubted His love for me, and I knew He was the only way and the One who could bring me out of this hole I had dug for myself. Ultimately, my problem was that I was reluctant to let Him live through me.

Months later, those days came to pass, and I thank God for His grace to stick with me through it. I would be a liar if I said I have not backslid from time to time throughout my spiritual journey in Christ. However, it seems the intervals of time between have been continually increasing. I drift less and less, and often for shorter and shorter periods of time. Transformation for me has been a process, but I know that day by day, He is renewing my mind and shaping me into the fully devoted follower He called me to be. The most important lesson for me through this transforming life is that there is a difference between living for Christ and letting Christ live through me.

Living for Christ is not the solution. There is too much ego in that mindset. When we think that all we need to do is live for Christ, we tend to measure our lives by our conduct. Yet our hearts can still be cold and full of deceit while doing the things that are deemed acceptable in the Christian experience. Though living for Christ is right, it is impossible to do so until Christ lives through us. I believe this is what the apostle John is teaching his readers when he wrote, "The love of God was made manifest among us, that God sent His only Son into the world, so that we might live through him" (1 John 4:9).

What is the difference between living for Christ and allowing Christ to live through us? When Jesus walked the earth, He lived through his Father in heaven. Though Jesus was fully God, He humbled Himself in His fully human condition, relying on His Father for all things. He said only what His Father had Him say and did only what His Father desired. His entire life was in submission to His Father. Though equal to God, He "did not consider equality with God something to be used to His own advantage" (Philippians 2:6, NIV). The Father lived through the Son.

When Christ spoke to His disciples on the night He was arrested, He assured them that His absence would be replaced by the presence of the Helper. Jesus told the men, "The Helper, the Holy Spirit, whom the Father will send in My name, he will teach you all things and bring to your remembrance all that I have said to you" (John 14:26). Christ lives through the Holy Spirit, just as the Father lives through the Son. The Holy Spirit lives through us, so that we can live through Christ. If that is what we hope to experience, Christ living through us, we must do as Christ did during his earthly ministry. We must count ourselves as nothing, "taking the form of a servant" (Philippians 2:7).

Though Christ was anything but nothing, for the sake of His Father, He made Himself nothing. No human has ever deserved to be something more than Christ deserved—being perfect in every way. Yet, Jesus understood what His Father had in store for Him and entrusted Himself to His Father and set Himself aside for His Father's glory. The Holy Spirit does the same in your life. It is His nature to be consistent, seeking the glory of Christ at work through God's creation. He will not fail nor become fatigued. He understands His purpose.

Do you entrust your life into the hands of Christ? Though "for freedom Christ has set us free," (Galatians 5:1), can you do as Christ did and humble yourself to the point where you say, and do only what Christ can do through you? He does not need you to do His work for Him, rather, He desires that you surrender your life to the point where He can live through you. Just as Christ made Himself nothing, we must also do the same. As believers, through the power and presence of the Holy Spirit, when we become nothing, He becomes everything to us. I believe this is what John meant when he wrote about believers living through Him.

Having the Advantage

"I tell you the truth: it is to your advantage that I go away, for if I do not go away, the Helper will not come to you. But if I go, I will send him to you." (John 16:7)

During the 1990s, I worked in youth ministry, involved in camp ministries, para-church ministries, and church ministries. Before I got married, I worked as an intern at a high-school church ministry in Fairfield, California. After getting married, my wife and I had a variety of experiences. First, we lived in British Columbia, Canada working at a Christian horse-ranch camp. Next, we moved to Washington state where we directed a summer day camp program in Bellingham, worked with Youth for Christ in Seattle, and directed junior high through college church ministry programs in Lynnwood. From there we moved to Arizona, where I served as a youth pastor in Glendale and then taught Sunday school for junior high and high school students in Peoria. These different positions gave me varied experiences in working with all types of teens. It was after this period that I became a police officer in 2000.

While in Washington, I got my first exposure to home-schooled Christian teens. They were part of a traveling competition team centered around scripture memory and made up 10 percent of the youth group. The oldest teens were very good, and they could quote large sections of scripture with ease. The younger teens really looked up to them. Their parents were extremely involved in their lives—overly involved in my opinion. As the Youth Pastor, the situation was unsettling for me because I struggled to connect with these teens who knew all the answers, (or at least all the verses). They didn't seem to need anything, nor could they be told anything; they projected near perfection.

Growing up, I was very independent at a young age. Early independence meant that I did a lot of stupid things and thought myself to be invincible. I did not hate authority nor reject it when it stood in front of me. However, I did a good job of avoiding it. As a youth pastor in my mid-to-late-twenties, I gravitated toward the searchers who were curious, yet skeptical. I could relate to them since I was one for quite some time. I learned early that my teaching style was more of an interrogation of scripture and wanted to help people discover its meaning for themselves.

When I taught, the kids on the memorization team (about 10 percent of the youth group) loved reading the verses, especially ones they had memorized. This small percentage of teens dominated the lessons, causing all the others to tune out. To keep the discussions interesting, I had to do something that made me unpopular. I put the memorizers on the spot and asked them to explain the meaning of what they read. They didn't have a clue; they didn't understand the words they had memorized. They couldn't see past the black print of the words on the pages—they wouldn't even try. This opened up a lane for the 90 percent to respond. The discussions got better every week.

What happened next, I should have seen coming. But I was too excited about the progress being made in reaching the unchurched teens. The home-schooled teens revolted, complaining to their parents about kids entering the youth room smelling like cigarette smoke and wearing dirty clothes. They complained about the language that they were hearing for the first time in their lives. They complained it was getting too crowded in the youth room. The parents brought their concerns to me, and the church leadership. I would not survive the campaign against me.

Seeing the writing on the wall, I called for a parent meeting to discuss the issues. I also invited the mother of one of the teens about whom they complained. She first came to me concerned that her daughter, Leanna, was suicidal. I met Leanna for coffee and invited her to our youth group. She showed up every week. As hard as I tried, I could not get anyone to connect with her. My heart conflicted every week Leanna showed up, knowing the message 10 percent of our group were sending her. I loved her and cared for her as best I could. After a few months, Leanna surrendered her heart to Christ.

At the parent's meeting, the concerned parents of the home-schooled teens aired their issues. When they finished, I asked Leanna's mom to speak. With grace and love, she stood, looked at the crowd of people, and told her daughter's story. She told the crowd that her daughter's life had been saved twice. She expressed gratitude to each parent, the church, and to me. She said she understood the parents' concerns and had heard similar views from others since her daughter was part of a dark crowd. I should note that Leanna's mother was not a churchgoer.

It was a turning point, with many tears in the room, but my heart was no longer there. I was disgusted. I left that ministry shortly after this event. I was embarrassed to be associated with any part of it. But I was a young man, perhaps still with much pride in my heart. And having brought pressure on me from the church leadership, I had given up all hope that these teens would ever get it. In my view, the home-schooled teens did not understand the working of the Holy Spirit in their lives and in the lives of others. My opinion was that all the scripture memorization in the world would not teach them how to love; that love must be practiced, not memorized.

Jesus knew that his disciples had not yet experienced the working of the Holy Spirit in their lives. The disciples thought they knew what was best: to keep Jesus around and have him handle business. But Jesus had other plans; the disciples would handle business for him. In the three years of Jesus' public ministry, the disciples had not yet learned how to love, although it wasn't their fault. They would soon learn how to love through the power of God in them—by the indwelling Holy Spirit who would come into their souls.

The home-schooled teens were coddled by their parents, shielded from the outside world, and unexposed to the smell of struggle. Would their parents be there for them for their whole lives? What would happen when they had to move on? To go to college, to get married, to live apart from such protection? On the other hand, Jesus had no intention of coddling His disciples. He would expose them to the dark corridors of life where struggle is inevitable, and pain would surround them. It is for this purpose that He called them.

Just before Jesus left the disciples, He assured them, "I tell you the truth: it is to your advantage that I go away, for if I do not go away, the Helper will not come to you. But if I go, I will send him to you" (John 16:7). He would go shortly after, and He did send the Holy Spirit, the Helper, and the Helper made all the difference in the world. Is there anything or anyone in this world you rely on more than the Holy Spirit? If so, you will not experience the full extent of His power working through you until you have released yourself from all other dependencies. It will be to your advantage that you let God be everything.

Turning the Tables on the Bankers
for the Beggars

"Truly, I say to you, the tax collectors and the prostitutes go into the kingdom of God before you." Matthew 21:31

During the final days of Jesus' public ministry, He entered Jerusalem for the Passover feast as an outsider. He grew up in Galilee, not Jerusalem, and His public ministry was mostly around the sea of Galilee, almost eighty miles away. Jesus visited Jerusalem a few times a year for the Jewish festivals. The streets in Jerusalem were swollen with people during these festivals as Jews from around the world entered the city. So, it would be relatively easy to go unnoticed.

The temple was the central hub during the festivals. During Passover week, people were required to offer a sacrifice. Packing light, affluent travelers likely preferred to purchase something to sacrifice at the temple. Of course, buying their sacrifice at the temple cost significantly more than if purchased elsewhere. Vendors capitalized on this and packed the temple platform that was filled with buyers. Much like the area around a crowded cruise port today, peddlers of all kinds transformed the temple base into a market. If someone had something to sell, the temple was the place to be. So, it is important to understand that the temple vendors were not just selling the required sacrifice.

As Jesus entered Jerusalem, He immediately went to the temple. Matthew writes that Jesus drove out both the sellers and the buyers. This is noteworthy because it was likely the only place wealthy travelers would find what they needed for their required sacrifice. To drive them out would leave many without an offering. Also, among the vendors were the moneychangers. Coming from all over the world, the well-to-do needed their currency exchanged to be able to buy anything. The moneychangers took advantage of their captive audience with an inflated exchange rate.

Jesus overturned the tables of the moneychangers (Matthew 21:12). Pushing them out of the temple would leave many, if not all foreigners without a way to purchase their required sacrifice. The vendors and moneychangers would be considered "essential businesses" by the government in Jerusalem. The Jewish people came to Jerusalem to celebrate the Passover. But with Jesus disrupting the purchase of the essentials, most people were left unprepared for the required sacrifice. I find this to be a very interesting and subtle point. It explains in part how and why the crowd turned from being enthusiastic at his Triumphant entry to being indignant of His existence.

Maybe it's just how I perceive this story, but I get the impression that the temple market was not a place for the poor but the rich. This market was not a place for the poor and helpless. Those who could afford to pay premium prices for a pigeon roamed the temple floor in a festive mood, spending money as if on vacation. Essentially, the Passover festival had become somewhat of a caste system—a separation of the haves from the have nots. Perhaps this is what Jesus observed as He entered the temple.

Yet in every society where rich people congregate, there are beggars nearby hoping to avail themselves of the rich's generosity. As Jesus overturned the market tables and disrupted the crowd, a group of beggars approached Jesus. They were the only people at the temple happy to see Him. The Bible does not record how many blind and lame came to Jesus, but Matthew wrote that Jesus healed them all (21:14). Praise the Lord! What a beautiful image of what Jesus was about. He showed no interest in the banker looking to capitalize on the required festival sacrifice. His attention was on the beggar, only able to collect spare change to pay for one more meal. Beggars didn't need to buy a pigeon for sacrifice. Nobody required it from them. They were marginalized, ignored, and neglected. Yet they were the focus of Jesus' ministry in Jerusalem.

Somebody would need to step up to confront Jesus for the sake of their economy, for the sake of their Passover celebration, and for the sake of peace. Agitating a crowd in overcrowded Jerusalem during one of the required feasts would draw unwanted attention from the Romans. Pilate was responsible for assuring the Jews maintained order during the feasts in Jerusalem. A negative report to the Emperor in Rome would be costly for Pilate. So, the chief priests and the scribes (also wealthy), hearing the healed cry out "Hosanna to the Son of David," were indignant. In their minds, the wrong people were celebrating.

They confronted Jesus, "Do you hear what they are saying?" (v. 16). Jesus heard them loud and clear. He knew the Jewish people had no desire for the truth—only the preservation of their religious system stimulated by the wealthy from all over the world. Jesus left the temple that day knowing that He would give His life even for those who rejected Him. I think it is fair to add that He understood that the marginalized, neglected, and the poor would be the ones who came to Him for the gift of life.

Jesus returned to Jerusalem the next morning and entered the temple once again. Were the moneychangers and the pigeon sellers back to business? The Scriptures do not inform us of this. Do you think they were? I do. But before Jesus could approach them, He was met by the chief priests and the elders of the people (v. 23). Jesus was teaching, likely to many of the same people He healed the day before. The poor and the needy were always the first people encountered approaching the temple. The elders interrupted Jesus' lesson with a challenge on His authority to teach. He dismissed their question, then incorporated the chief priests and the elders into His lesson.

Jesus gave a short parable, likely one that the chief priests and the elders couldn't understand but that the poor and marginalized could see: A man had two sons and asked them to work in his vineyard. One son said he would but did not work in the vineyard. The other son refused, then worked in the vineyard. Which of the two sons obeyed the will of their father? The elders answered correctly, the second son. It is here that Jesus makes His point, "Truly, I say to you, the tax collectors and the prostitutes go into the kingdom of God before you" (v:31).

Jesus cleverly asked a question to force the elders to testify against themselves. Jesus' point here is that the religious leaders rejected Him. But the prostitutes and tax collectors believed in Him and repented, thus doing the will of the Father. Applying this lesson today, I wonder if we have neglected the needy for the sake of our celebrations. I wonder if we have become more like the elders and less like the tax-collectors. I wonder if there is any gain in this. I wonder who is fighting to keep Jesus' message alive or if His message has lost its purpose.

Jesus disrupted the Passover celebration. The chief priests and elders spent many days and weeks planning for the festival, only to see Jesus throw it into disorder, draw negative attention from the Romans, and attract many more beggars to the temple. The religious preferred the space be kept available for those with money to spend. But they got

239

crowded out by a crowd of people who actually needed Jesus. Do you need Jesus, or do you just need a place to celebrate?

A Police Officer's Love

"Greater love has no one than this, that someone lay down his life for his friends" (John 15:13)

According to statistics reported to the FBI, 89 law enforcement officers were killed in line-of-duty incidents in 2019. Of those, 48 officers died due to felonious acts (Offenders used firearms to kill 44 of the 48 victim officers), and 41 officers died in accidents, either vehicle accidents or training accidents. The average age of the 89 officers killed in 2019 was 40. During my years in law enforcement, our department has laid to rest 17 men who lost their lives in the line of duty, 12 the result of an attack against the officer. Many other officers have died while still with our department, whether by suicide, sicknesses, or traffic fatalities while off duty.

At the time of this writing, July 6, 2020, this year there have been 116 line-of-duty deaths nationally. 51 of those deaths are from the COVID-19 virus. Though COVID-19 is no respecter of one's occupation, what is notable is that those deaths are mostly the result of men and women exposing themselves to the invisible coronavirus while doing their job, serving others in vulnerable environments.

I have attended many funerals for police officers during my career. During most of those funerals, the words of Christ to His disciples were spoken about the fallen officer: "Greater love has no one than this, that someone lay down his life for his friends." I have also attended many funerals for fellow believers in Christ throughout my life. I find it ironic that I have yet to hear this passage quoted at a believer's funeral to memorialize how the believer lived. I know there have been many who have lost their lives for the cause of Christ. Those men and women personify the meaning of this passage. But I just personally have not witnessed it at a funeral.

A few years ago, I attended an in-service training session. I cannot remember the training topic, but the instructor said something that has been on the edge of my mind ever since. He said, "Don't die for no good reason. If this job is going to take your life, make it for a good cause." I believe the instructor's words resonate with Jesus' intent with His disciples.

He was preparing the disciples for their mission, to bring the gospel to the world. For doing so, Jesus made it clear to them that they would be hated, put out of the synagogues, and their lives would be threatened (John 16:1&2). To those men and women who accepted Christ's words and mission, His words to them then still stand today: they are the men and women who express the greatest love one can have for another.

It is noteworthy to me that Jesus told His disciples that such love to friends is the greatest expression one can show another. But what about such love for strangers? How about for enemies? A police officer accepts the call to go where nobody wants to be. The radio call of an emergency or a crime in progress is enough to move any officer into the path of danger. The color of one's skin is not a factor, nor is the socio-economic status of the one in need. During that moment, one's sexual identity, political affiliation, religious background, or personal ideology is not the officer's concern. The police officer will sometimes get the call from home while sleeping or at a restaurant in the middle of a well-deserved dinner break (and they will still pay for the food they don't have the chance to eat).

Only about one-tenth of one percent of police officers tarnish the badge in this country. The rest of these fine men and women live up to such a high calling that they deserve the recognition as those who love to the greatest extent. They model it. Though these days have challenged the integrity of the badge and the polyester cloth worn by all officers, they continue to dress out with honor and distinction. Police officers are under assault, unlike any time I have ever experienced. Politicians exploit them for their political gain. Citizens have attacked them for their selfish gain. And churches have ignored them, perhaps in fear of retaliation, retribution, or for self-preservation. Yet officers continue to do their job, knowing well the risks associated with it.

Perhaps that's why such love is seen as the greatest one can have. It is a love for one another, even strangers and enemies, knowing that such love could cost one his or her life. It is an understanding that some causes are worth dying for, though nobody wants to die. The police officer does not want to die for a stranger. They want to go home and be with those who love back. They want to take a deep breath and enjoy those for whom they have sacrificed so much. They don't respond to emergencies out of haste. He or she has trained for this moment. Decisions are made well in advance, long before they get to the call.

Is the officer perfect? Far from it. There are so many variables to consider in the flash of a moment. They do not have the luxury of writing out a speech to a husband and wife in the middle of a dispute, nor to a subject wielding a knife at a crowd. Yet they find words to say, hoping for the best outcome for all. When the officer succeeds, nobody is around to compliment the good speech or the wise words. The officer is rewarded with another call to go to. If the officer does well for the day, they get to go home.

What is the reason for my writing this? I am taking a few minutes of my time and yours to express my sincere appreciation for those who have accepted the call. I am one of the lucky people in this country, as I get to witness such love every day through the men and women I am surrounded by. They have earned the opportunity to wear the badge and express such love. We, the church, must stand by them, for if we lose them, there may be no one left in this world who knows how to love to such an extent. Let's not wait for another officer to have to lose his or her life in the line of duty so we can honor that officer with the distinction of such great love referenced by Christ. Let us learn from them, walk with them, and love like them.

Source: https://www.fbi.gov/news/pressrel/press-releases/fbi-releases-2019statistics-on-law-enforcement-officers-killed-in-the-line-of-duty

When God's Men are Men of God

"The authorities are God's servants, sent for your good. But if you are doing wrong, of course, you should be afraid, for they have the power to punish you. They are God's servants, sent for the very purpose of punishing those who do what is wrong" (Romans 13:4, NLT)

A concern I have heard from many of my fellow police officers is that they no longer feel welcome in public settings—any public settings—including church. Many Christian police officers believe the church is too polarized today and that the divide is being ignored. Christians are not exempt from using social media as a platform to state strong opinions, and anyone can see that not all Christians support police officers. Many times, pastors will speak out against divisive speech on social media but say very little to address the perception that police officers are systemically racist or abusive in their power or authority. As a result, police officers are walking away from the church.

Previously, attending church was a haven for an officer—a safe place where one didn't have to look over their shoulder, worry about a confrontation, or listen to opinions of their profession. That safe place has been lost. What if your profession was under scrutiny, and was being discussed in coffee circles at your church—would you still attend?

Many career employees view what they do as a calling and recognize their service as a noble cause for society. However, would a brain surgeon feel comfortable doing the work of a steelworker on a skyscraper? Likewise, would an untrained person feel comfortable doing the work of a Christian missionary in a dangerous country? Probably not. Yet police officers, especially those with a faith foundation understand that they are engaged in a noble cause, doing what is best for society. They feel called to do work nobody else wants to do, running towards danger in critical moments. It is unfortunate that many church leaders and members have taken polarizing and public positions regarding 21st Century policing, in step with society's cynicism toward those who serve in uniform. Ask your pastor if he would be willing to deliver a sermon in support of those who are called by God as Paul outlined. What do you think their response would be?

It is not my intent to ignore injustices in society through blind loyalty for police officers. I do, however, wonder why this profession is singled out more than others. I cannot think of any other job in this country that does more screening, testing, and vetting than police departments for their hiring process. A candidate's qualifications alone should be enough to give them the benefit of the doubt. On the job, police officers often make split-second decisions that could drastically alter their lives, and they make those decisions well almost every day. When they fail to make the right decision, they are accountable and are held responsible. Though at times an officer may make a mistake of the mind, they rarely make mistakes of the heart.

As you read the passage above, do Paul's words to the church in Rome bother you a bit? Do you cringe when you read that pagan government authorities were the avengers of God's wrath to the wrongdoer? Do you view police officers as God's servants, sent for the good of society? Would God use non-believers to execute His justice for the good of a civil society? I am certain that Paul's words to the Romans are relevant to us today. During my tenure in law enforcement, I have seen both extremes—from the universal support that all police officers received after 9/11 to endless consternation, accusation, doubt, and concern over the competence of today's police officers. Violence against police is on the rise. With all that is going on in society today, one question must be resolved: Are all police officers given authority by God to punish the wrongdoers in society?

To answer this question, a bit of background may be helpful. Paul wrote the book of Romans to a group of believers he did not personally know since he had not yet been to Rome. The church was likely started by some from Rome who were in Jerusalem on the day of Pentecost (Acts 2). Despite not having the benefit of apostolic teaching, the church grew doctrinally sound. Unlike many of the books Paul wrote to the churches, he did not correct doctrinal issues with the church in Rome. Paul's purpose in writing to the Roman Christians was to provide solid doctrine mixed with practical instruction, something all churches still benefit from.

Paul's letter to the Romans covers a great deal of doctrine; in fact, this letter is one of the most exhaustive studies on the righteousness that comes from God found anywhere in the Bible. The letter lacked historical references to current issues the Roman church was facing. However, Paul wrote this letter from Corinth. While in Corinth, he worked closely with a married couple, Aquila and Priscilla, who came to Corinth from Rome to minister for the gospel after Rome declared Christianity illegal. Aquila and Priscilla were likely influential in informing Paul about the Roman church and encouraged him to write to the Christians still in Rome.

Though the Roman government was increasingly hostile toward Christians, Paul wrote, "Everyone must submit to governing authorities. For all authority comes from God, and those in positions of authority have been placed there by God" (Romans 13:1). Paul demanded that the Roman Christians view government officials as servants of God. They may not have been men of God, but they were God's men, placed in position by God. That's right. The pagan authorities who opposed Christianity in Rome were placed there by God, and the only thing to do about it was to submit to their God-given authority, respect the rule of law, and live quiet lives. They were not to live riotous, defaming lives, nor were they to rebel against those in positions of authority.

This concept that pagan officials were referred to as God's servants was not a new idea. The pagan Babylonian king, Nebuchadnezzar, was called God's servant (Jeremiah 27:6). During his reign, the Babylonians laid siege to Jerusalem and eventually captured the city, destroying the great Temple and the city walls. He was God's servant to punish the rebellious Israelites and take the people in captivity to Babylon. The pagan Median Emperor, Cyrus, was called God's anointed shepherd (Isaiah 44:28). God used Cyrus to issue a decree that the captive Jews could return to the Promised Land. Even Jesus said to Pontius Pilate, "You would have no power over me if it were not given to you from above" (John 19:11). The man responsible for issuing the death decree against Jesus was given the authority from God to do so.

These are a few examples throughout the Bible of leaders who may not have been men of God, but they were God's men. I believe this is the context in which Paul writes to the Romans. Furthermore, Paul adds that resistance against the authorities is resistance against God, and such actions incur judgment (Romans 13:2). Is Paul instructing the Roman church not to resist the government? I believe he is. But what if the government is unjust? Should we not resist an unjust government?

First, do so at your own risk, and expect consequences for your actions.

Second, America is one of the few exceptions in the history of the world where resistance against the government is tolerable at all. In the United States, the framers wanted citizens to have the right to petition against the government when the government exercised abuse of power, but such a petition was to be civil.

Third, I do not doubt that governments are altogether better when men and women of God are in positions of authority. Consider the influence Joseph had in Egypt, or that Daniel had in Babylon, or that Esther had in Persia. I also do not doubt that policing would be better if the positions were held by men and women of God. But that is just not the way it is.

Police officers are ministers of God (Romans 13:6). They may not all be men and women of God, but they are all God's men and women. It is time that Christian churches everywhere recognize the God-given authority of police officers as ministers of God. It is time for society to back away from the accusations, generalizations, and judgments made against all who wear the badge. When a pastor fails morally, it is not an acceptable conclusion that all pastors are immoral. The fallen pastor must account for his failure. Likewise, the only police officers who should be subject to judgment are those who have tarnished their badge. Even they must face 'the servants of God, avengers who carry out God's wrath on the wrongdoer."

I believe society needs more Christian police officers and that local churches should be more intentional in honoring those who wear the badge, recognizing them as servants of God. I believe more should be done to guard the hearts of law enforcement men and women at home, including their church home. I also think that church leaders should learn from them, to best understand the culture they serve. Finally, it is unbecoming for a police officer to defend his honor. They do not need society's approval to do their job. But if we want officers to participate in serving in the church, then we must defend their honor for them.

Tough Skin, Tender Heart Part 2:
Leaders Forfeit Their Right to be Offended

"It may be that the Lord will repay me with good for his cursing today" (II Samuel 16:12)

I do not recall a section of training in the police academy on how police must endure continuous insults while doing their job. However, there is no doubt that any who choose this career are well aware that insults come with the job. How, then, can police officers prepare themselves for constant abuse? Let's be honest, if you were subjected to constant insults while at your job, just for doing your job, eventually, you would probably reach a tipping point. Maybe you would resign from your position and find less contentious employment. Maybe you would complain to your boss about your work conditions. Maybe you would file a formal complaint against another for creating a hostile work environment.

Most would say that insults come with the job in law enforcement, so an officer must overcome such a hostile environment. I would agree. But it makes me wonder what makes police officers better than average citizens in their capacity to be abused daily? How can they continue to be professional without letting the insults become personal? I am not suggesting police officers are better people. However, the public should realize that police officers are ordinary people with an extraordinary ability to not take offense when insulted. In 2021, If an officer takes offense and reacts with hostility, that officer will be looking for a new job.

Unfortunately, I can't offer examples of insults I hear on the streets; they are too offensive to repeat. But I do not need to give examples because turning on the television news shows what officers endure. You can see and hear it for yourself. You may have already taken notice of these men and women showing remarkable restraint while doing their job. Perhaps you have commented on it, saying, "I don't know how officers can stand there and take it." Civilian friends comment to me about how hard it must be to see things that officers see. Most commonly they state that they would not be able to take the constant abuse.

Here lies a principal worthy of reflection: Leaders must forfeit their right to be offended. We all have the right to take offense. Some get offended quite easily and often. People like this can be difficult to be around because it's like walking on eggshells speaking with them. We all have someone like this in our life that comes to mind. But leaders must make decisions every time they hear offensive words. Words can be quite offensive, no doubt about it. But do they have to be offensive? Words can only offend when we allow them to.

Consider the power we have when we offend someone; we can diminish another person with just our words. But one can't be an effective leader if mere words can destroy them. In reality, words spoken have no power—the power lies in their offense. If leaders choose not to take words offensively, then the offender is powerless, and the leader retains his power, authority, integrity, and reputation. A thin-skinned leader is not an effective leader.

As you read this, you probably take no offense at what I am saying. However, based on experience, I find that the people in the U.S. that get the most offended by words are Christians. Does that offend you? I find that some of the most thin-skinned people are pastors and leaders in the church. They seem unable to be subjected to criticism or insults. If a pastor is insulted, the insulter is considered divisive and often is shunned or avoided. However, insults cannot divide unless the church leader affords himself the right to be offended.

Likewise, how often do people leave a church because they feel offended? Why should anyone give that power to someone else, to run them out of their church? When that happens, the insulter retains the power and becomes stronger. The only resolution is not to take offense, thus rendering the insulter powerless. Is this too high a standard to expect at church? I hope not.

Christians must be tough-skinned yet retain a tender heart. I have a daily reminder of this at home. It's a portrait of a grizzly bear looking at the tip of its nose, watching a monarch butterfly rest there. The bear possesses so much power, yet its tender heart admires the butterfly, and the butterfly feels safe.

King David, a man after God's heart, possessed this balance. A low point in his life was when one of his sons was mounting a coup against him. King David fled his city, and with him went thousands of his loyal followers. They left because David did not want any of them to be injured or killed when his son raided the city. David was so distraught by this that he left barefoot, weeping as his people ascended the Mount of Olives to the East. Arriving at the top of the Mount, David encountered a man from the tribe of Benjamin who hated him. He hated David because he had claimed the throne from Saul, a Benjaminite.

The man shouted insults at David, mocking him for his son's overthrow of his kingdom. He threw rocks at David and kicked dust in his face. David's loyal men stood at his defense, willing to cut the head off this man who dared to insult the king of Israel. But David said to his loyal men, "Behold, my own son seeks my life; how much more now may this Benjaminite! Leave him alone, and let him curse, for the Lord has told him to" (II Samuel 16:11). David was broken and humbled by his son's betrayal, and he accepted the betrayal as having come from the hand of God. This man's insults paled in comparison to what David's son had done, yet he accepted his circumstances humbly. "Let him curse," said David.

As David led his people through this problem, he added, "It may be that the Lord will look on the wrong done to me, and that the Lord will repay me with good for his cursing today" (v. 12). Then again, maybe not. I love David's perspective here. He left the consequences of this man's insults to God, and he left the outcome for himself to God. No false promises or blind faith are needed here. David took the power from this man and trusted the All-Powerful to deal with him.

David continued toward the Jordan while the man walked along the opposite hillside continually cursing him, throwing stones at him, and kicking dust. David proved himself to be a leader. He did not look for pity from his loyal followers. He understood that they, too, were being subjected to insults. At face value, it may look like weakness on David's part. But David actually demonstrated great strength. He took the power away from the insulter. He continued toward the Jordan to refresh his followers. David forfeited his right to be offended.

Are you easily or frequently offended? I believe our calling is to have a tender heart, but the only way we can guard that heart is through a tough skin. Discovering the balance between tough skin and a tender heart is difficult. Many police officers have tough skin, but their hearts are hardened through their experiences. Unlike King David, they lack balance.

A tender heart is a life-long pursuit and to achieve it, one's skin must be thick. I believe this is our calling as Christians.

First, Remember Who You Are

"For do I not know that I am this day king over Israel?" (II Samuel 19:22b)

After more than twenty years in law enforcement, I have a better understanding of how my actions, personally and professionally, reflect on the police department I work for. On occasion, I will receive a commendation for an investigation worked. For new officers, receiving a commendation is a big deal. It goes into your personnel file for review when being considered for transfers or a promotion. All commendations have a typical format; first, a narrative of the event. Second, a description of a particular action taken by the officer that is commendable. Third, a statement of how the officer's actions mirror the highest standards and practices of the police department. Ultimately, it is this final statement in all commendations that matters most.

Does what you do or say matter to anyone? If so, who is most impacted by the decisions you make, good or bad? Have you ever done something that poorly reflects on someone else or an organization? As a police officer, one poor decision is broadcast on news networks across the country. Investigation of the officer may go on for days or months. Such scrutiny is a heavy burden to carry through life. Yet only a small number each year fail to live up to the highest standards and practices established by their departments—a testament to the solid work done every day across this country by 800,000 police officers. It is commendable how well men and women who wear the badge face extreme scrutiny of their conduct. And they do this while under the uncertainty of exceedingly hostile conditions.

Is there a standard like this in the Christian church today? Are Christians trained to live up to the highest standards and practices of community expectations? Often times, outsiders to the church say that Christians are just hypocrites to explain what they perceive as non-Christian actions or behaviors. But within the church, it is common to hear Christians say that nobody is perfect to justify a lower standard. So, whether looking from the outside or the inside, I think it is fair to say that Christians generally do not have a high standard for themselves.

If there should be a set of high standards in the church, what should apply? Is perfection expected? Obviously Not. Even those outside the church do not expect Christians to be flawless. However, what do they expect? Well, they expect that we live like Christians. Whether we choose to accept this or not, our identity comes with some expectations. Just as police officers represent the department they work for, Christians represent the church. Police officers can uphold the highest standards of their profession. But they may struggle in their personal life, for example, in their marriage. Society does not judge police officers for such struggles. They understand and often empathize. So, why does society often judge Christians differently?

I believe there should be some universal standards of expectation from within the Christian community. Not to be confused with high morals, these standards require consistent practice. They should always be for the good of others and represent the church. But they are impossible standards to keep. Instead, consider them disciplines. Just as an officer should never take offense at an insult, Christians should not either. In practical terms, all expectations of police officers should also apply to Christians.

I previously mentioned a Bible story about a man who insulted King David. He took advantage of perceived weakness as David humbly withdrew from Jerusalem to avoid a coup by his son Absalom. The man followed David away from the city, assuming his reign had come to an end. However, after Absalom died in battle, David returned to Jerusalem and his rightful throne. How do you think that man felt now? He likely thought that the restored King David would have him killed since it was clear that he had not been loyal.

Thinking his fate was sealed, the man, named Shimei, quickly weighed his options. He realized he had insulted the wrong man. But Shimei also knew that King David was known by all as a humble, principled man, with a heart like God's. Shimei "hurried to come down" (v. 16) to meet King David. As difficult as this was for Shimei, he knew it was best to go to David before David sent for him. He brought with him a thousand men from his tribe, probably to demonstrate that he was a leader and influencer among his people. Shimei likely reasoned that his influence would assure the king that all among his tribe pledged their loyalty.

Shimei approached the king and said, "I have come this day to meet my lord the king" (v. 20). David's guardsmen, who were also insulted by Shimei as they fled Jerusalem, suggested to David that they kill him. But King David said, "do I not know that I am this day king over Israel?" (v. 22). He then gave an oath to Shimei, telling him he would not die (v. 23). In other words, David represented his people. He knew he must do what was right. Furthermore, David was king by divine appointment. Therefore, David knew he had to follow what God called him to do.

Here is the principle of this story: Before you take any action, remember who you are and who you represent. When you take no offense at an insult, you represent God. When you forgive, you represent God. When you show mercy, you represent God. When you love, you represent God. You know what God has done for you (John 3:16). You know that He takes no offense at your sin. You know God forgives. You know He is merciful. You know you are loved. So, you are capable of these things, too. Not to the extent that God is because your love cannot save another. However, you can stand when insulted without taking offense.

These are just a few of the standards and practices that Christians should uphold. When done extraordinarily well, they are to be commended. Commendation in this case is the encouragement to keep up the good work. These are high standards, but they are not impossible standards. They can be lived up to, with focus, determination, and discipline. Let us be known as Christians, not because we attend a church, but because we live up to our identity in Christ.

Has Justice Disappeared?

"So the law is paralyzed, and justice never goes forth. For the wicked surround the righteous; so justice goes forth perverted" (Habakkuk 1:4)

I read a news story about a man who was indicted on rape charges in 2019. Now in 2020, his lawyers argued that he should be released while awaiting trial because the COVID-19 virus endangered both inmates and their attorneys. He was released on a $25,000 bond over the objections of a prosecutor. Upon his release, he tracked down his rape victim and shot and killed her. When located by police, the man crashed his car then shot himself.

Unfortunately, stories like this have become so common that we rarely experience shock or grief over the injustices we hear about or witness. As a detective, it is exasperating to track down the same suspects we previously arrested and charged with major crimes and then have to find them again due to new felonies committed while released and awaiting trial. Is justice something we can expect in this world?

As previously mentioned, I was once a detective assigned to our Repeat Offender Unit. I worked as a liaison between the county attorney's office and the police department to ensure that certified repeat offenders received enhanced prison sentences. My responsibilities included testifying against defendants at sentencing hearings. I had to explain my rationale as to what made each defendant a Repeat Offender. There were a number of salient characteristics considered before making such a determination. Experience concluded that behavior was predictable if people lived consistently under certain circumstances, such as drug usage, unemployment, transient lifestyle, and recidivism.

At one particular hearing, the defendant was young, probably nineteen years old. Police had multiple felony charges against the young man over the span of a few months. He was a burglar who was committing three to four residential burglaries every day. He did not have prior prison time due to his age. The county attorney asked that I explain to the judge why the young man should be given a prison sentence. I told the judge, "Your honor, upon this young man's release, he will reoffend within a day." I explained why and I believed I had made a good argument. The judge wanted the young man to be given another chance. He sentenced him to limited jail time with work release and put him on probation. On his first day of work release, he never returned. That same week, we worked on new cases of burglaries involving this young man and had to arrest him again on new charges.

What can be done in an unjust society? How does God process such injustices? The prophet, Habakkuk, wrote about this very same issue about 2600 years ago. Habakkuk was witnessing the decay of the nation of Judah and the rise of the Babylonian Empire. The Babylonians overthrew the Assyrian Empire and were working their way toward Jerusalem. Judah's godly king, Josiah, was killed during the chaos of the invasion. Josiah's three sons and grandson succeeded as king, but all of them were worthless. During Josiah's reign, Judah had made significant spiritual reforms, but all this progress was erased by his successors.

The nation quickly reverted back to its corrupt ways. Though the royals lived well, the people suffered immensely. Idol worship was common, and decency could not be found anywhere. Habakkuk wondered why God was so silent and how He could allow His chosen people to get away with such corruption. The prophet believed God should punish the people in order to purge the evil and restore the nation. Perhaps Habakkuk's concern is your concern today.

How did we, as a nation, get to this point? How could the events in Portland, Oregon continue without local government intervention? Why does it seem like right is wrong, and wrong is right? Regardless of one's political leaning, how could anyone justify such violence and destruction? Where is God in all this? I believe that what we are witnessing today is similar to what Habakkuk saw, and his question to God seems to be our question to God: Where are you in all this? Habakkuk cried out for divine intervention, as we do today.

God's response to Habakkuk was that He was sending the Babylonians to Judah for judgment, to destroy the city. Not satisfied with God's response, Habakkuk asked God why He wouldn't just purge His people and restore their righteousness. It didn't seem right to Habakkuk that a nation more corrupt than Judah could prevail against them. Though God promised to punish Babylon for their corruption as well, Habakkuk had his own theological understandings, and what he heard from God did not make sense. He struggled to understand God's purposes.

Dissatisfied with what he was hearing, Habakkuk took a different approach with God, arguing that God owed it to Himself to defend the Jewish nation, to vindicate His character, and keep His covenant promises. Habakkuk asked God, "why do you idly look at traitors and remain silent when the wicked swallows up the man more righteous than he?" (1:13).

The book is short, just three chapters. But by the end, Habakkuk realized that God is not just someone we worship because He blesses those He loves. He is Someone to be worshipped no matter what because God is God. Habakkuk's final words are worth repeating: "Though the fig tree should not blossom, nor fruit be on the vines, the produce of the olive fail and the fields yield no food, the flock be cut off from the fold and there be no herd in the stalls, yet I will rejoice in the Lord; I will take joy in the God of my salvation" (3:17-18).

Habakkuk did not ignore the troubling times or the injustices he witnessed. He did not conclude that everything was OK and dismiss the difficulties with some trivial responses. Habakkuk asked some hard questions and changed his understanding, and confronted one of his theological obstacles, that God had His hand in all the difficulties. He is not a passive, nor silent God. He is not "hands-off" in Portland. Though these are difficult days and may get worse, God has not turned away.

Those who believe that God's kingdom on earth in this present age will make the earth a better place may need to read Habakkuk again. If that is what you believe, what will you say if things continue to get worse? Rather than trying to force current events into the belief that "if Christians were more influential in society, society will improve," why not change like Habakkuk did and conclude that salvation is more than just a better life on earth? God's kingdom is firmly established, and Christ Jesus reigns. He has overcome this troubling world, and He will fulfill every promise He has made. We can rejoice in the fact that King Jesus is in control, even if it appears as though Portland is not.

"God, the Lord, is my strength; He makes my feet like the deer's; He makes me tread on my high places" (3:19). May we resolve to see beyond the chaos and confusion in society and look at the broader perspective that He is enough. Let us pursue what is right and just, and never what is evil and unjust. However, let's not lose our focus. The righteous shall still live by faith.

Habakkuk is considered one of the minor prophets, yet when I read the book, I realize that the audience he was speaking to was himself. Perhaps Habakkuk continued in his prophetic ministry, yet we have no record of his continued messages as we do with Jeremiah during the same time. But what I love about this book is Habakkuk's honest frustration and the progression of his understanding to trust God over all our circumstances, even the ones that do not seem fair.

Are things going well for you? Are you a pastor in a church and struggling to reclaim your congregation after the COVID-19 fall-out? Are you unemployed due to the restrictions placed upon your work? Have you been denied something you believed you deserved, like a funeral for a loved one, a wedding ceremony, or a church to attend? Have you had a family member hospitalized but were unable to visit? Are you concerned that your government may defund or dismantle the police, leaving you and your family vulnerable to anarchy and random violence? I see no benefits to denying the struggle. It is real. However, regardless of our circumstances, each large or small problem, and every benefit or blessing, has been and will be first sifted through the loving hands of God for His approval before they reach us. Take comfort in this and trust Him. He is not silent, but that does not mean He is not subtle.

So, rather than asking God for an easier life, pray for the strength to live through a difficult one, and trust Jesus when He said He has overcome the world (John 16:33).

Turn

"Truly, I say to you, unless you turn and become like children, you will never enter the kingdom of God" (Matthew 18:3)

If you work hard for something, putting in your best effort, you should be able to get what you worked for. That principle makes sense to us, right? We are conditioned to think that way from childhood. Our parents, teachers, and elders told us we can be anything we want if we set our minds to it, work hard, and never give up. So, it is our nature to believe that. And I believe that principle is true for the most part. It is fair and sensible and rewards effort. If you work hard for something, and another doesn't even try, why should the other be given what you have pursued?

The pursuit of religion is not much different. Many of us have been conditioned to believe that the harder people work on disciplines like morality, devotion, humility, and kindness, the greater the reward should be for their effort. That's logical in the minds of people and consistent with the way many of us have been taught. We tend to size up others in this way, spiritually, by comparing others to ourselves. If I read my Bible every day, I must be more devoted than people who read their Bible once a month. If I am more kind than you, I must be more spiritual than you. This is a common way of thinking, regardless of our religion.

Did Jesus teach this principle? That those who work the hardest for something should get more than those who do not? There are examples of Jesus teaching the virtues of hard work, dedication, and persistence, but did He teach that salvation is a reward given to those who work hard for it? Jesus taught His followers that their reward would be great, but what will they be rewarded for? If salvation is not a reward, how can one be saved? Are there any requirements for mankind to be saved? Yes! To be saved, we must agree first that we cannot save ourselves. Then, we must discover the way to salvation through Jesus Christ and turn to Him for eternal life, trusting that by turning to Christ, we will be saved.

Christianity is unique from all other religions, primarily in two ways. First, Christianity is all about the person of Christ Jesus. It is a relational pursuit. Because it is relational, it requires some level of communication, covenant, and devotion. Because Christ lives does not mean I know Him.

I live on the same street as my neighbor five houses down, but I do not have a relationship with him, and I do not know him. Though we are neighbors, we are not connected. Likewise, going to church does not mean one knows Christ. He may be there, but that does not mean everyone there knows Him. First, we must establish a relationship with Him. No other religion is based on a personal relationship with a savior.

Second, Christianity promises salvation by grace through faith and rejects the notion that we can earn it. For Christians, it is impossible to live in such a way that we eventually deserve to go to heaven. However, all other religions teach that salvation is based on merit. Followers of other religions are motivated to do more or be more spiritual as a path to salvation. Christians must avoid this merit-based thinking. Those who believe they will earn eternal life through personal accomplishment are merely practicing a religion that cannot and will not save.

Some may feel a sense of conviction that their lives are not in order. As a remedy, some go to church hoping their attendance will relieve their regrets or troubles. They listen to the messages and try to apply some of the moral lessons, hoping to get their lives in order and become better people. If they remain in church long enough, thinking this way, they may believe they evolved into becoming Christian. This line of reasoning is more common than church leaders would like to believe. And when people get to that place in their lives, they do not understand that they are living a Christian lifestyle without knowing Christ. If they were honest with themself, they would admit something is missing in their life, and the deepest longing they hoped to fill still exists in their heart.

If such hard work, dedication, and consistency cannot save a man, how is that fair? If Jesus had not provided a clear path for salvation, that would be unfair. However, Jesus stated the solution clearly and emphatically, "unless you turn and become like children, you will never enter the kingdom of God." Consider your life and your motives. Be honest with yourself and ask, "Am I hoping to save myself?" Do you only trust in yourself for salvation? If you are placing trust in your own effort, are you at peace?

We all desire inner peace. We all are in pursuit to fill the deepest longing in our hearts. We sense the emptiness and pursue all we can to fill it with a sense of purpose or pleasure. But nothing really satisfies over time, whether fame, fortune, or good health. We know there is more. By the goodness of God, we were all created with this longing.

Jesus has the solution: Stop trying to save yourself! Judiciously, Jesus accomplished everything needed to resolve the separation between God and mankind. Jesus is the solution, the remedy, the cure, and the antidote. He is everything and has provided everything. He initiated and accomplished all the requirements God demands to bring us into a relationship with Him. So, does that mean everyone has been saved? No. Though the work is complete, Jesus spoke to the whole world when He said, "unless you turn, you will never enter the kingdom of God."

To turn is to agree with God that you cannot save yourself. To turn is to acknowledge that you are on a collision course without Christ, and the inevitable result is death. To turn is to concede that Jesus Christ is the only solution to your problem and the emptiness in your heart. To turn is to reject your own way of salvation, thinking that if you try hard enough and become good enough, you deserve eternal life. To turn is to humble yourself and look to Christ for forgiveness and redemption. To turn is to forever let go of the belief that we must do our part to keep our salvation. And to turn is to be convinced that He will do everything He promised and save us. Every promise made by God is a promise kept.

To turn is to have complete and total confidence in Christ that He has saved you. To turn is to start over, as a child, as a new creation, in a new relationship, dependent on Christ for all things, knowing He provides all things. Finally, to turn is to relinquish control over your own life, presenting Christ with the greatest gift you can offer: your complete and total self—your heart, mind, soul, and strength. This is not done blindly, but with the confidence that comes through faith that He will meet all your needs, get you through all your troubles, and give you peace and the abundant life He promised.

You must turn to experience the abundant life He promises. But it is not a life of fame and fortune—those are not important. And it is not a life of ease and comfort—those are not guaranteed. It is a life with purpose that streams through the relationship with a living Savior, Christ Jesus. It is nothing to give Him everything you have. Because, by turning, you become convinced that you have everything you need.

Is this a fair exchange? Those who try their hardest to save themselves won't. But those who stop trying to save themselves and look to the only Source of life will be saved. Is that fair? The Giver of life has provided the means for eternal life. But why did He give up His life to save others, yet not save everyone? I believe it is because He is relational, by nature, and wants to enjoy those who want to enjoy Him. It is impossible to have a relationship any other way. Christ's love is a gift that one must desire. Though painful to God, He loves His creation enough to not force anything on them. He does not give people a life they do not want.

Those who try to save themselves can certainly try to do that. However, God will nudge them frequently and insert others into their lives who point them to The Way. But He will not impose His will on anyone who rejects His offer for salvation and insists on living independently from Him. To all, one important question must be asked: Have you 'turned?' If not, are you still hoping to save yourself? Stop! It is not worth the pursuit. You will never have peace this way. Kneel before Christ and receive the gift He offers you. It is the only way to experience peace and the only way to receive eternal life.

Discovering Your Potential

"Now to Him who is able to do far more abundantly than all that we ask or think, according to the power at work within us" (Ephesians 3:20)

If you have children that played sports as they were growing up, you have likely witnessed a dad in the bleachers who kept yelling at his son or daughter to try harder. The dad shouted instructions, criticized their child's effort, and demanded them to give it everything they had. You probably cringed when you heard this and wished the father would just sit down and remain quiet like the rest of the parents. You probably felt embarrassed for that child on the field who had to hear their dad's voice above all the other parents, relentlessly pushing for more.

On the other side of the bleachers, perhaps you have heard a mother cheering on her son or daughter for anything her child did on the field. If the sport were soccer, the mom cheered for her child if they touched the ball as it incidentally rolled in their direction, regardless of whether the child made a play on the ball. At the end of the game, the mom filled her child with praise for simply being on the field.

If you have seen this, you may have noticed the irony here. More often than not, the best player on the field had the loud father, and the worst player on the field had the over-celebratory mom. Both were somewhat annoying and disturbing to sit through. To be fair to both parents, the dad knows his child is very good at the sport, and the mom knows her child is not. However, neither approach from either parent is helpful to the child.

When the apostle Paul wrote a letter to the Ephesian church, he was careful to articulate and highlight the many spiritual blessings received in Christ. Here is a summary of these blessings. He has: blessed us in Christ, chose us in Him, predestined us in love, adopted us as sons, redeemed us through His blood, forgiven us for our sins, made known to us the mystery of His will, united us to Him, reserved for us an inheritance, given us hope, sealed us with the promised Holy Spirit, and guaranteed His promises to us (v. 1:3-14). Take some time to reflect on these spiritual blessings lavished on us from our King and Savior.

As a result of these blessings, Paul reminded the believers that they have access to Him, and we should approach Him with confidence (v.

3:12). Paul understood that for the people of God to make known to the world the wisdom of God, they must first understand their identity in Christ. To fail to know who we are is to fail to live up to who we are. God tells us the truth of who we are and challenges us to discover it.

How does God challenge us to discover our identity in Christ? He fills us with Himself and lets us explore the potential we each have within us. Paul prays for the Ephesians that they may discover the strength of God's fullness. He prays that they may perceive Christ dwelling in their hearts. He prays that the believers may find the deep roots Christ has established in us to keep us and to strengthen us and that they may experience this strength and make sense of it. Paul concludes his prayer with these words, "To Him who is able to do far more abundantly than all that we ask or think, according to the power at work within us" (v. 3:20).

I know God is able—I can fill in the blank from here. What can God not do? He cannot create anything larger than Himself. He cannot create a rock that He cannot move. He cannot create another being that is greater than Himself. He cannot create a problem that He cannot resolve. He cannot create a virus that He cannot manage. The creation can never be greater than the Creator. So, as I read Paul's words, that God is able to do far more abundantly than all that we ask or think, we need to put that phrase in a proper context.

Paul stated that God is able to exceed our expectations of what we think He can do through us. The Creator of the universe can simply say something into existence. "Let there be light," and there was light. What can God do through me? He can make Himself known to others through me. He can display His power through me. He can heal another through me. He can pierce a man's heart through me. He can reach the whole world with the glorious message of the gospel through me. But does God need to yell at me, to try to convince me that I can do more or that I can be better? No. Does He need to lie to me and tell me I am great when I am not? No. Neither of these approaches will help me discover the power of His presence working through me.

God invites me to find the power of His presence in me. He wants me to study His "sport," to know how to play it, and practice continuously. God knows that if I do practice, I will discover His potential within me. Are you filled with all the fullness of God? That was Paul's prayer to the Ephesian

Christians (3:19). Paul knew that if we seek to know God and the power of His presence in us, His plan will be made known through us. And Paul knew that if we understand our identity in Christ that is guaranteed for us, we might allow His purpose to be made known through us.

After reading through this passage, I cannot help but wonder if the power of Christ in us is for us or for others who have yet to experience Him. God's plan for mankind is to build a Church, make Himself known to the Church, resulting in the Church making God known to others. The Creator of the Universe has recruited a team, and every person on the team is ready to play, possessing the power to move mountains. When the Church makes known to the world the wisdom of God, the world experiences the power of God. However, and tragically, could it be that God's wisdom and power are rarely seen by the world because God's people either are not aware of it or they want to keep it for themselves?

A Testimony

"For what we proclaim is not ourselves, but Jesus Christ as Lord" (II Corinthians 4:5)

I am fortunate to be working on what I believe is arguably the most effective and efficient crime suppression entity in our country. Referred to as the Crime Impact Unit, it consists of three squads, totaling about twenty-five detectives from our police department. Our mission is to identify, locate, track, investigate, and arrest the most violent criminal offenders in our city. Our strategy is to confront offenders when they least expect it. We wait for the most opportune moment to approach an offender, which allows us to control their movements and avoid deadly-force encounters.

In 2020, our unit made 754 arrests involving violent criminal offenders. Included were high-profile investigations: homicides, armed robberies, shootings, stabbings, car-jackings, rapes, kidnappings, weapons violations, and unspeakable crimes against children. The men and women who are on this detail are highly trained, highly motivated, tactically sound, and equipped with exceptional investigative skills. Together, we authored 259 search warrants to assist in our mission. Body warrants, GPS tracking warrants, phone locating warrants, and evidence recovery warrants are also essential skills we used in conducting investigations efficiently.

Though these statistics are impressive in terms of crime suppression, they do not give the whole picture. Considering the violence potential of every person arrested by our unit, we had zero officer-involved shootings in 2020. This statistic is remarkable because over eighty of our arrests were made when the offender was armed with a handgun. Also significant is that these are 2020 statistics, a year where homicides increased in our city by over 50%. 2020 was a year wrought with obstacles for the law enforcement community. Yet the Crime Impact Unit's assistance to the Homicide Bureau led to a higher percentage of cleared cases from previous years, a 72% clearance rate (Chicago's was 44.5%). A cleared case results from the totality of evidence brought forward for the successful prosecution of a suspect.

It is also noteworthy that our unit cannot be defined by a specific incident or any one detective who outshined the others. To me, this equates to reaching the pinnacle of crime prevention, because as individuals, our identities have faded. Individually, none of us are special, unique, or better than any other officer. However, together we have lived up to what we were called to accomplish.

What is my point in running down these statistics? These results are due to the consistent and persistent work of the Crime Impact Unit doing what it was brought together to do. All of our work was performed against the backdrop of an increase in violent crime nationwide. Some of our work was performed in culturally hostile environments between communities and their local police precincts. And we worked with limited personal contact with witnesses due to COVID-19 restrictions. No individual accomplishments nor a single high-profile incident resolved could highlight the significance of 2020's results. More than that, every violent offender took off the streets by our detail meant less contact with patrol officers incidentally running into these subjects on routine traffic stops. Therefore, the results of this unit's efforts are a testament to the drive, dedication, and purpose of its existence. Every day, night and day, without taking time to celebrate our last arrest, we push forward to the next predator that needs to come off the streets. It is a testament to the character and talent of each individual, working together to make up the unit.

So, what do I mean by "testament?" Well, a testament, or testimony, is a statement given based on eye-witness experience and observation. In a courtroom, a jury considers the credibility of a witness based on the witness's personal observations. The jury must determine if a particular witness has first or secondhand information during their testimony. In the same way, your testimony is your eye-witness account to the new life you have in Christ. It is not a recounting of a historical event that you believe. That is considered secondhand information. In a court of law, that testimony would be dismissed by a jury. However, whatever has been personally experienced cannot be disputed or nullified. Think of it this way: there is only one person that can testify on your behalf that you are saved, and it is you. If you do not believe that you have been saved, try convincing someone else that you have. It's impossible. However, if you have experienced the peace and life promised from above, your testimony cannot be disputed.

Have you ever heard a person give their Christian testimony? A typical testimony has three components to it. First, a starting point, by mentioning life before and without Christ. Next, how and when they became a Christian. Then, a conclusion with a brief synopsis of how their life is better or different now. This is a typical testimony, not because it is the best format, but because it seems to be the most logical way to tell a story. But what are we really highlighting here? How does one's experience speak of Christ? What if the person's life became more difficult after their conversion? What if the person lost their job, their spouse, and their friends after coming to Christ? How does that story compel others to be Christ-followers? Telling others that life is easier because we are saved can be misleading and inaccurate.

In the apostle Paul's second letter to the Corinthians, he writes, "For what we proclaim is not ourselves, but Jesus Christ as Lord" (II Corinthians 4:5). By our testimony we proclaim our eye-witness account of Christ in us, working through us. It's the power of God, who can do all things through Christ in us, transforming us into Himself progressively and intentionally. But God's work in us is not complete until He comes again and restores us perfectly. Only then do we obtain righteousness.

Our testimony began when we experienced the conviction of sin and the realization that we were destined for destruction—deservedly. The turning point in our testimony was when we discovered the remedy to our problem. Christ came and dwelt among us. He lived and died according to God's plan of salvation for His creation. Jesus then returned to life, defeating the death penalty so that we would never experience it.

Our testimony is a running narrative of the progression of this transformation from death to life. Our story has no end since our transformed lives are being renewed every day as God continues to reveal Himself to us. We discover who we are as His children and gain a continually deeper understanding of what He did and what He suffered to save us. We learn how to listen closely and respond quicker. For every promise we find in Scripture, we have an opportunity to grow in our faith by believing those promises and trusting the One who made them.

Our testimony is an eye-witness account of the power of Christ to save what was lost. But if we were never lost, how can we give an accounting of our redemption? We can't. Accordingly, our testimony is not about our discovery of Christ but His recovery of us. It is about His knowledge of who we are and what we have done. It is about His forgiveness, remarkable as it is since He sees everything. It is about His plan, implemented through our lives. Each day we learn to put aside our agenda for the sake of His, in us and through us.

Frankly, our testimony should be pretty impressive. But I hope that as you read through this, you were not more impressed by the crime suppression statistics than you are with the mighty work of God in the lives of His chosen every single day—because our society is in desperate need of His testimony, not ours.

Living Condition Yellow

"Always be prepared to make a defense to anyone who asks for a reason for the hope that is in you" (I Peter 3:15)

For law enforcement officers, it is advantageous to know a suspect's state of mind when approaching them. When dealing with a violent criminal who has already committed a dangerous offense, it is ideal to approach them in their most relaxed state. Relaxed criminals create an advantage for an arrest team. They increase the likelihood of an effective detention and keep everyone from harm and injury. Part of my assignment within the law enforcement community is to watch and follow violent criminal offenders. I wait for them to relax and then call in an arrest team. The team can now approach the criminal with the element of surprise.

People generally reside in one of four conditions:

Condition White: This is the most relaxed state, essentially unaware. When we refer to someone in Condition White, they are generally unaware of their surroundings. They are calm, and they do not have their guard up. They are going about their daily business. Metaphorically, they are sheep grazing in a pasture. Most people live their lives in a state of condition white. Even criminals, after committing a violent crime, eventually fall into this condition. Whether they take a trip to the local convenience store or go for a swim at a public pool, their guard is down. It is optimal for police to approach criminals when they are in this condition. Unfortunately, the mere presence of a marked police vehicle or a uniformed officer can quickly escalate a criminal's state of mind.

Condition Yellow: Every police officer lives continuously in Condition Yellow. Everybody knows that police like to see the door at the restaurant when they are eating. They are aware of their surroundings and prepared to respond to whatever may happen. They are observing, yet relaxed. Officers train themselves to respond, imagining scenarios everywhere they go. They look around for secondary exits, notice the bulge of a concealed weapon, pay attention to body language, and listen closely to interactions. Metaphorically, officers are the sheepdog watching as the sheep graze. Condition Yellow is the state citizens are in when driving, and they see a police vehicle behind them—cautious. Criminals are the same, and in this state of mind, they are ready to make a move if they feel threatened or exposed.

Condition Orange: In this condition, an officer is ready to respond to an imminent threat. Most training scenarios, whether in combat or tactics, are in this state of mind. As an example, let's say police are called to a burglar alarm in the middle of the night and find an open door. They may enter with weapons drawn but in a low-ready position, meaning their guns are pointed down at a forty-five-degree angle. The officers will proceed to clear the building. If the officers see a threat, they are ready to respond quickly. In another scenario, suppose an off-duty officer is in a restaurant and is suspicious of someone who enters. He sees the silhouette of a handgun under a T-shirt, and the person is looking around nervously. The officer instantly goes into Condition Orange. He will get up and move into a tactical position. He will watch closely. If the person poses no threat, the officer returns to Condition Yellow as if nothing happened. Essentially, the off-duty officer senses Condition Orange in another. Metaphorically, it's the sheepdog watching the wolf on a hilltop as the wolf looks down on the sheep.

Condition Red: This is the combat condition. It's the bank robber with his gun drawn at the teller or the police officer in pursuit. It is a dangerous time for everyone and is absolutely the worst time for officers when dealing with a criminal offender. The criminal will fight or flee every time. There is no higher state of mind. Again, metaphorically, it is the moment of attack between the wolf and sheep. The sheep, the wolf, and the sheepdog are all in Condition Red. Panic, aggression, and uncertainty of outcome are their respective responses.

So, what is the point? Looking at I Peter 3:15, I believe Peter is teaching that as followers of Christ, we should all be living in a state of Condition Yellow. When this verse is broken down into smaller parts, there are seven notable components to it:

First, "always be prepared." To live Condition Yellow, one must be prepared for almost anything. Those prepared to respond are more likely to have an adequate response in the moment. There is no advantage in life to be oblivious to the world around you. From the perspective of the follower of Christ, this condition is an enhanced sense of others. Social scientists refer to this as an increased Emotional Intelligence.

Second, we should live prepared "to make a defense." We get the word Apologetics from this passage. It means making a defense of the faith, not an apology for it. A follower of Christ needs the training to have a response ready for the most commonly asked questions in life. Does your church train you for this? It is impossible to simply listen to someone talk about a topic and believe that counts as life preparation. There must be an interactive environment where followers can practice defending their faith in Christ. Jesus taught His disciples. He then sent them out to apply what they had learned and to see the results for themselves. This allowed His disciples to learn about themselves, discover their strengths and weaknesses, identify areas for improvement, and reassess their approach. If the church offered this type of training to followers, maybe we would become more confident in making a defense.

Third, we should always be prepared to make a defense "to anyone." Let's face it; if we live in a confined relational box with limited exposure to strangers, friends, family, and work associates, "anyone" is easy. Many who live in such confines often argue that they have already done this, as though they have checked off this box in life. If this is the case in your life, let me encourage you to live in a bigger world. Go to more places where you can meet more people. Live exposed enough so that people may approach you. When they do, be prepared to make a defense.

Fourth, always be prepared to make a defense to anyone "who asks." Nobody appreciates having religious tracts tossed in their face when they are walking down the street. No one cares for someone at their door on a Saturday telling them how sinful they are. These tactics are rude and unproductive. But when you live in Condition Yellow, people will notice. They will see how you position yourself to respond to their needs. They will recognize your readiness. They will ask. However, don't expect to be asked to defend your faith in Jesus if you live in Condition White.

Fifth, always be prepared to make a defense to anyone who asks, "for a reason." Why are you a Christian? Can you answer that question in a way that makes sense? Do you fumble over your words when asked? Can you articulate what you believe? If you lack training to do this, more than likely, you will not do this well. If one asks you for your phone number, does it make you nervous to recite it? Are you confident that the numbers you give someone are accurate and in the correct order? Of course, you are. So, why is it that we get so nervous when asked by someone why we are Christian? Is that a hard question to answer? Living Condition Yellow means we are ready to respond to the "why" questions people may ask.

Sixth, always be prepared to make a defense to anyone who asks for a reason "for the hope." Do you believe the message of the Gospel is a message of hope? If so, it is not necessary to scare Hell out of people to share Heaven with them. Hope describes the peace and life we have in Christ. It is absent in those who are perishing, and if they are honest with themselves, they will admit it. Hope describes the certainty of our life in Christ. In other words, hope is the confidence we have in His Promises. We cannot speak of the forgiveness of Christ if we struggle to believe in His forgiveness toward us. I believe the hope of eternal life is contagious because God has created the human heart to only be satisfied by His presence.

Finally, always be prepared to make a defense to anyone who asks for a reason for the hope "that is in you." To those who receive Jesus, He gives the gift of eternal life. He then seals that life with His Holy Spirit, guaranteeing our inheritance. As we come to know Him more, we discover the power of His Presence through our lives, power that comes from Him. This should be noticeable! It should draw attention. So, when people are drawn to ask, it is not the story about your life that people need to hear. Instead, it is the story of Christ, the redeemer of mankind through the forgiveness of sins that we must be prepared to talk about.

What do you think it looks like to live in an elevated state of mind? Training develops our mindset, preparing us for what we practice for. When we train for situations, we enable our bodies to activate muscle memory rather than instinct. We respond rather than react because we are already in an elevated state of mind, thus prepared for possibilities. We find ourselves recognizing situations before they overcome us. It's like dodging a punch because you see it coming rather than getting sucker punched. I believe this is the essence of the passage we have looked at. By living in a perpetual state of Condition Yellow, you will be ready to respond as the Lord initiates contact with others. Consider how you can train for this.

He Was One of Us

"Have this mind among yourselves, which is yours in Christ Jesus who, though he was in the form of God, did not count equality with God a thing to be grasped, but emptied himself, by taking the form of a servant, being born in the likeness of men" (Philippians 2:5-7)

A pastor, police officer, crack addict, and a prostitute walk into a bar together. Sounds like the first line of a typical dirty joke. However, when you read that, what questions come to your mind? Why are they together? Why are they walking into a bar? Which one do you think is out of place?

Analyzing this scenario, each of the four is subject to the scrutiny of other bar patrons for being in a bar and being with each other. Some may think a pastor should not be in a bar; someone from his church may see him (or he may see them), and he is with a prostitute! If the police officer sits down with a crack addict and a prostitute, the assumption is that he is corrupt. The crack addict may be perceived as a snitch for being with the police officer. And some might think the prostitute is trying to entrap potential clients by being with the police officer.

In this scenario, it is plain to see that the perception of others is the biggest obstacle all four would face. But what if the four were friends with one another? What if they were getting together to celebrate the police officer's promotion to detective at the end of his last shift on patrol? Does this seem impossible to imagine? What if they were all siblings? Does that change your perspective?

When we see the unexpected, we naturally form an opinion. But learning the circumstances of what we see can radically change our perspective. I would not have expected to see the Creator of the universe nestled in a manger, a mere feeding trough. I would not have imagined Him surrounded by hay, feed, and animal dung, in a small unfamiliar village far from home. Would you? He's better than that. He deserves better than that. I had something better than that, and likely, you did, too.

I certainly would have never thought that the tax collectors and prostitutes would feel more comfortable around Jesus than the religious elites. After all, He was perfect, and so were the Pharisees (or so they thought). I have always been told that people are not comfortable around perfect people, yet the prostitute wanted to be by Jesus' side. How did Jesus do that? Perhaps more importantly, why don't the marginalized of society feel comfortable around us, or us around them?

If other's opinions did not matter to us, perhaps we would invest more in the dirty, the broken, and the immoral. Or would we? The perception of us by others is only one obstacle we face. We still need the desire to be with them, relate to them, and become one of them. Yet even that is not enough. They must see us as one of them. Looking back at the cartoon on the cover, what do a prostitute, crack addict, and a police officer have in common?

Three obvious observations can be made. First, proximity: They are coming toward one another. The police officer comes down the street and starts to roll down his window. He knows the area as though he expects to run into some familiar faces. As he approaches the two walking, they stop and turn toward the officer. Usually, the sight of a patrol car in this area has people going in the opposite direction. Second, comfort: The two walking know the officer's name—one waves, the other smiles. The officer approaches from the driver's side of his vehicle, a vulnerable position for a cop. Third, friendship: Every person in this cartoon is taking a relational risk. They are in public. The crack addict and the prostitute will be asked by those watching what the officer wanted. Their relationship with the officer will make others nervous. But friends are not influenced by the perceptions of others. A friend is the one who considers another of greater value than oneself. Friends should have no social class separating them.

Truth be told, Jesus was one of them. Not sinners like them but rejects like them. Have you noticed that most homeless people tend to live in a relatively small part of their city? Why is that? If you were a transient, would you not instead go to an area where there is less competition for spare change? No. You would remain around people who understand you best. People who know when you are hurting just by the way you walk into the soup kitchen. People who know your story. Perhaps Jesus was comforted by those who were poorest. Maybe he felt that they understood.

When Jesus became one of us, which one of us did he want to be like? Do you think when he got old enough to understand who he was and what he was to do, that he was disappointed with his upbringing? He had a poor father who died before he could see his son's life and ministry. His widowed mother raised her children alone. His siblings resented him because his mom reminded him every day of who he was. Neighbors mocked him and refused to embrace him as the Messiah.

Jesus became one of us, one of the broken, one of the humbled, one of the hurting. No wonder it is the broken who can see best who He was, the Chosen One, the Savior. He rescued me when I was a broken man in need of a Savior. He came to me, and I saw Him as I was: broken. He befriended me, and I felt at peace when He was with me. I wanted to be with Him more and more, and then I wanted to be just like Him. I wanted to go where He would go and do what He would do. I discovered that He spent a lot of time with broken people, and He loved them. He identified with them, and I came to know Him more and more as I fell in love with broken people. He became one of us, so that we could become one of them. Roll your window down.

Acknowledgments

This book would never have happened had it not been for Gary Morgan. His conviction was that others could benefit from the perspective we shared during numerous hikes along Arizona's desert trails. I would not have put all this together in book format. Gary has no experience in publishing books, but he learned how to do it, and he rallied people around him who could help. To be honest, I pretty much stayed out of the whole process, contributing on occasion from my observations as I read through Scripture.

Gary shared some of these devotionals with other men to review once he tackled the editing. Gary focused on grammar and offered suggestions when he felt I had not completed my thoughts. The men he shared these pieces with reviewed them for relevance. When Gary received helpful feedback from people I do not know, I concluded that we had something worth reading. To those who read through these devotionals and provided feedback, I thank you as well.

For a final editorial eye, Gary turned each chapter over to Larry Bohlender, a retired college professor and newspaper editor. I am grateful for the special attention Larry gave each piece, knowing it had already passed through others' eyes, yet still seeing changes that needed to be made.

I have a very close friend, Scott Harris, who has been meeting with me regularly for the last 23 years. He has been a steady presence and has kept me balanced and focused. It is rare to have a friend to walk side by side with for so many years. I am a better man for it, and I am sure many of my thoughts and perspectives on these pages were vetted by him before I wrote them.

I want to thank all the people I have shared a portion of my life with who have given me experiences and viewpoints worth mentioning in this book. My church experiences have not all been positive nor negative, but I have learned lessons from many of them. Life on the streets as a detective has not always been easy, but I have seen the world as it really is, and these experiences have added color to my daily Scripture reading. Family life has not always been easy. Sharing a home with others has its ups and downs but having the opportunity to share it with people who have shaped me is deeply appreciated. I am grateful for the lessons learned and the people who were a part of those stories.

My wife, Nicole, of almost thirty years, has been a steady presence in my life. She has made the rough waters much easier to bear. We married before I entered law enforcement, but after I came to know Christ. She has loved me like no other and has been asked to read many of these devotionals over the years. Thank you for being honest with me when I did not make sense. And thank you for reminding me to complete my goal from almost thirty years ago, to write a book.

For you who are reading this book, thank you. I have asked myself ten thousand times why anyone would take the time to read my thoughts. I hope you might see why I believe this book is different from the many others you may have read. I hope this book either renews your passion for life or gives you some perspective to muscle through the obstacles you face.

Finally, I thank God that He breathed life into me and promised to sustain me until the end. Almost every day for more than twenty years, I have prayed a simple prayer:

"Lord, I do not know what I will see or do today, nor do I know where I will go, nor when I will be home. But I do know that every experience in my life has first been shifted through your mighty hands and has been approved for my good and your glory. Give me enough just for today. I will be back tomorrow morning for more."

Receive the glory, for you are worthy.

About the Author

Jim Ferree has been a sworn officer of the Phoenix Police Department since 1999 and has served as a detective since 2005. For most of his career, he has been assigned to a street detail, working in a plainclothes capacity. He has had the privilege of working beside some of the best detectives, officers, and supervisors in the department; most of whom helped shape his perspective on humanity, humility, and integrity.

He received two undergraduate degrees from Briercrest College in preparation for full-time Christian ministry and served as a youth pastor for most of the '90s. After transitioning to law enforcement, Jim earned a Master of Science in Leadership from Grand Canyon University.

He recognized a call to ministry early in his Christian journey but had no idea how God would shape that calling to place him where he serves today. Jim is average in every way, just like the rest of us, and that is what makes his writing style so relatable. He thinks about the things people struggle with. Though he would say he hates giving advice, his perspective has proven to be helpful to the many men he has mentored over the years.

Jim has been married to Nicole for almost thirty years. Jim credits Nicole with keeping him grounded in his faith through difficult times and readily acknowledges the sacrifices she has made to keep their marriage alive. They have two adult children who will always be the apple of their eye.